in

Westchester

and

Fairfield Counties

in

Westchester

and

Fairfield Counties

A nature lover's guide
to 36 parks and sanctuaries

KATHERINE S. ANDERSON

REVISED AND EXPANDED BY

PEGGY TURCO

Backcountry Publications
Woodstock · Vermont

An invitation to the reader

If you find that conditions have changed along these walks, please let the author and publisher know so that corrections may be made in future printings. Address all correspondence to:

Editor, Walks and Rambles Series, Backcountry Guides, PO Box 748, Woodstock, Vermont 05091

Library of Congress Cataloging-in-Publication Data
Anderson, Katherine S., 1926–1988
Walks & rambles in Westchester and Fairfield counties: a nature lover's guide to 36 parks & sanctuaries/Katherine S. Anderson; revised by Peggy Turco.
p.   cm. — (Walks and rambles series)
ISBN 0-88150-277-4
1. Walking—New York (State)—Westchester County—Guidebooks. 2. Walking—Connecticut—Fairfield County—Guidebooks. 3. Natural history—New York (State)—Westchester County. 4. Natural history—Connecticut—Fairfield County. 5. Westchester County (N.Y.)—Description and travel. 6. Fairfield County (Conn.)—Description and travel. I. Turco, Peggy. II. Title. III. Title: Walks and rambles in Westchester and Fairfield counties. IV. Series: Walks & rambles guide.
GV199.42.N652W473   1993
796.5'1'09747277—dc20   93-29152
CIP

© 1986 by Katherine S. Anderson, © 1993 by Peggy Turco

Second Edition, 1993

10   9   8   7

Published by Backcountry Guides, a division of The Countryman Press, PO Box 748, Woodstock, Vermont 05091
Distributed by W.W. Norton & Company, Inc., 500 Fifth Avenue, New York, New York 10110
Printed in the United States of America

Design by Sally Sherman
Maps and calligraphy by Alex Wallach
Cover photo © 1990 by Joel B. Dyer, courtesy of The Nature Conservancy
Photographs on pages 145, 160, 166, 181, and 186 by Peggy Turco
All other photographs by Katherine S. Anderson
Line drawings by Pamela Anderson

Twenty-four of these walks were originally published in *The North County News,* Yorktown, New York. They are printed here in revised form, with permission.

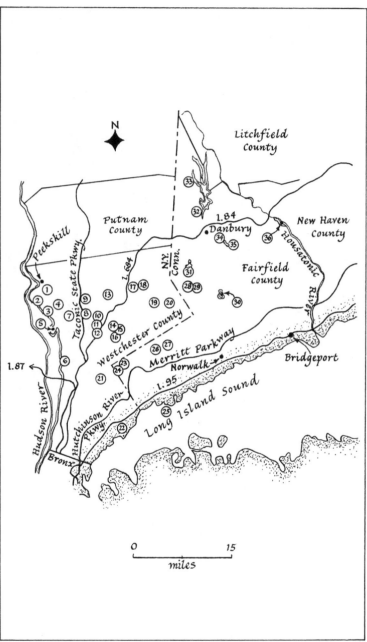

N

Litchfield
County

Putnam
County

Peekskill

New Haven
County

I.84
Danbury

Fairfield
county

Taconic State Pkwy.

N.Y.
Conn.

I.684

Hudson River

Westchester County

Merritt Parkway

Bridgeport

I.87

Norwalk

Bronx

Hutchinson River Pkwy.

I.95

Long Island Sound

0   15
miles

Contents

Foreword

Walks and Rambles in Westchester and Fairfield Counties was first published in 1986. The book was a hit, which came as no surprise to admirers of its author, Katherine Anderson. In the years that followed publication, thousands of people used its descriptions of woodland pathways, flora, and fauna to find new enjoyment in wild places within an hour's drive of downtown Manhattan. All who picked up the book were fortunate. The author, a naturalist for the Saw Mill River Audubon Society, knew the wildlife and wild places of Westchester and Fairfield counties better than any other naturalist. She was the recipient of numerous awards, and when she retired from active teaching, fellow naturalists from throughout the area covered by this volume gathered to present her with a plaque for meritorious service. Never was an honor more richly deserved or more enthusiastically bestowed.

Two years after the book's publication, I presented Katherine Anderson—an old and much-loved friend of mine—with a stack of writing tablets. The idea was to spur Kaye, as friends knew her, to begin writing a sequel or a revision or anything she chose to put on paper. Sadly, fate intervened. Two weeks later the best all-around field naturalist I have ever known was dead of cancer.

Walks and Rambles, then, is especially precious. It represents the voice of Katherine Anderson in its only surviving form, a voice that, during a long career as a professional naturalist, instilled a love of nature and a boundless interest in the outdoors in countless children, teenagers, and adults. Those who knew Kaye can find her here, leading them along a favorite footpath as in days gone by; those who never met her—I imagine they will constitute the majority of readers—can benefit from her wisdom and enthusiasm.

The idea for the book came from a column called "Walk With Me," which Kaye wrote for a local newspaper. Never much of a self-promoter, Kaye was strongly encouraged to rework the original essays into a book. We are fortunate that she allowed herself to be persuaded.

In time, every book becomes dated in one way or another. This is especially true of walking guides. Paths are rerouted, ponds dry up, meadows turn into woodlands, and fires and insect infestations convert dark, primeval glades into sunny clearings. We are doubly fortunate, then, to have this revision of *Walks and Rambles*. Peggy Turco has gone back to the trails, checked them for changes, and rewritten the text where new conditions demanded revisions. Peggy, the author of *Walks and Rambles in Dutchess and Putnam Counties*, was well suited for the job. The present volume is the result.

Edward Kanze, June 1993

Revision Author's Introduction

In this revision of *Walks and Rambles in Westchester and Fairfield Counties,* Katherine Anderson's walk designs and commentary have been kept intact, except where trails or plants have changed or disappeared. In several places new information has been inserted, especially regarding local history, ecology, folklore, and Native American place-names and culture. The book also contains six new walks in Fairfield County. Two of these—Paugussett and Pootatuck state forests—are hikes that you will need the larger part of a day to complete.

Despite the state boundary that separates the two, Westchester and Fairfield counties share similar characteristics. An animal or plant you read about and encounter in Fairfield County will most likely also be found in Westchester County. You can think of the two as being one giant and continuous living laboratory for the walker-naturalist. These two counties are bounded by major rivers, Long Island Sound to the south, and the inland hills to the north. Both counties lie within the eastern deciduous woodland biome of North America and contain plant communities that are, to a certain extent, predictable according to soil type. One expects to find oak forests on the crests; a mixed association of oak, tulip tree, sugar maple, beech, black birch, and shagbark hickory can be found on the slopes; red maple and ash grow in the swamps; cattail and phragmites are found in the freshwater marshes; and spartina grasses grow in the salt marshes. Hemlock grows in cool ravines and on sheltered moist flats, north-facing slopes, and ridge-top pockets. Both counties share the same geology and are mostly part of the same metamorphic, Early Paleozoic, New England granitic-gneiss complex that begins in Manhattan and stretches southeastward. Small sections of the northern part of Westchester and the northwesternmost part of Fairfield are part of the older, Precambrian, Hudson Highlands granitic-gneiss group.

Both counties share similar patterns of human history and historic land use. For thousands of years, both counties were occupied by

Algonquian-speaking Native Peoples. The various Lenape groups of the Hudson Valley and Long Island shore were, in some cases, closely related to the various Paugussett peoples of the Housatonic Valley. By the 1800s the early Dutch and English had clear-cut the landscape for farming and fuel. Both counties today share a similar degree of agricultural abandonment and pressure for industrial and housing development. Their natural systems suffer under the same stresses of pollution and change wrought by introduced flora and fauna. The most recent and notable of these influences, perhaps, is the woolly adelgid insect that is destroying the hemlock groves and is forecast to cause great change in the landscape. Yet change is what ecosystems are all about; a static ecosystem will not survive for long.

Perhaps only one natural feature separates these two counties. Most of Westchester County lies within the Hudson Valley watershed and is bordered by the tidal estuary of the Hudson River. Much of Fairfield County drains in the opposite direction to the Housatonic River. Both, however, border Long Island Sound, a truly special resource with limited public access. Some rivers in both counties drain directly into the sound. The Hudson and Housatonic rivers and the Long Island Sound moderate the temperature of the surrounding landscape, which, therefore, shares a similar climate; lands bordering the sound, the Hudson, and the Housatonic are somewhat warmer year-round than the inland hills.

This work is not an exhaustive compilation of parks in the two counties; there are many more properties in which to walk than are described here. But by reading this book and visiting the sites, the reader should get a feeling for the heartbeat of the land and an appreciation of its plants and animals.

Peggy Turco, 1992

Map Legend

parking area	Ⓟ
main trail	● ● ● ●
side trail or alternate route	. . . .
point of interest	X
fields	⬭
marsh	⚘ ⚘
building	■
bridge	⊨
cemetery	†
boardwalk	● ● ● ●
trail boundary	● ● ●│● ● ●
boulder	⏶
point of elevation	▲
corduroy bridge/logs	●‖‖‖‖●
stone wall	⨯⨯⨯⨯⨯⨯
view	⁄↓ᐸ
vegetation border	⌒⌒⌒⌒

Introduction to the 1986 Edition

D espite the rapid growth of housing, shopping malls, and corporate world headquarters, Westchester and Fairfield counties have within their borders many areas that retain the flavor of the wilderness that once was here. Thirty of these places have been gathered in this book. This is not a book of hikes, but a book of gentle walks (which is not to say that there are no hills to climb or rocks to scramble over). They are offered with the hope that they will refresh your spirit as they increase your knowledge of the natural world.

Sizes of the properties vary from six acres to almost five thousand acres. Larger places, such as Ward Pound Ridge Reservation and Devil's Den, have many other trails besides those covered here. You can obtain complete area maps when you visit them. Whether called park, preserve, sanctuary, or reservation, the lands described herein are considered protected against exploitation of any plant or animal. There is much here for you to enjoy, because the people who came before you have left the wilderness virtually intact.

Most of the places in this book are open from dawn to dusk. Trails are usually open even on days when nature centers are closed. A few areas, primarily the Westchester County parks, charge nominal parking fees. Camping is available at only two of the parks, Croton Point and Ward Pound Ridge Reservation.

The walks in this book are organized in a west-to-east sequence, starting at the Hudson River and ending in Fairfield County, Connecticut. You may wish to follow more than one walk in places where they are close together. For example, Graff Sanctuary and Croton Point, both in Croton, make a nice combination. In Chappaqua, Pinecliff Sanctuary and Choate Sanctuary or Gedney Brook Sanctuary could be visited in one day. In Redding, a longer walk at Huntington State Park might be followed by a shorter walk and a picnic at Putnam Memorial Park.

Many of the organizations that maintain these sanctuaries are composed primarily of volunteers. For that reason, you will not find trails in pristine condition at all times. In addition, nature is always making changes—a particular wildflower is replaced with another species, trees are downed in storms, and so on. You might like to add a small pair of clippers to your backpack and give a hand to some of the workers. Even in county and state parks, maintenance is very often the last item in the budget.

Most trail markings are painted on trees (paint is more difficult to vandalize than plastic or metal markers). Markings vary. The Appalachian Trail system (three dots indicating the beginning or end of a trail, two indicating a turn coming up) is used by many places. Others, including Pierrepont State Park, use simple white bands painted around the trees. (See the legend at the end of this introduction for other map information.)

You know how you like to dress for walking. Nevertheless, it is important to mention the need for adequate gear. Concealed, slippery roots, rolling rocks, or inadequately cut spikes of saplings can cause trouble, so wear appropriate footwear. (It is also advisable to carry an ace bandage in your pack.) Some people like to hike in shorts in warm weather. Long pants, however, will offer more protection from mosquito bites, ticks, and the all-pervasive poison ivy. From shad flies in early spring to deer flies in summer and mosquitoes almost anytime, some kind of nuisance insect is almost always with us. Many people like to use repellents, and some find that hats are helpful. You will soon discover what works best for you.

As far as equipment is concerned, your own interests will dictate. A hand lens will add immeasurably to your pleasure. Binoculars can be used for distant botanizing as well as for watching birds. Field guides are always helpful, especially if your companions carry different ones from yours.

My friends and I have a saying, "Never leave home without your lunch." Certainly, a high-energy snack is a good idea; so is water, particularly during hot weather. Be sure someone knows where you are going and when you expect to return, especially if you like to walk alone.

I have tried to discuss something of particular interest at each location described in this book. However, since many of these woodlands are similar, you will meet old friends in every one. Where registry boxes exist, it is helpful to property managers if you enter your name. You might also note any interesting sightings that other people would like to share. Because the laws of the state of New York require these lands to be used for educational purposes, it is important for property managers to know how many people take advantage of the woodlands.

My thanks to the many friends who have helped me explore these walks and to my three children, without whom the book would never have been written. Special thanks to my editor, Susan Edwards, from whom I learned so much during our months of work together.

> "...they do not die poorest who have helped to add one gleam of healthy pleasure to the lives of their fellow creatures, or increased by one tiny grain the sum total of human knowledge."

—Richard Kearton, 1902, from the introduction to the sixth edition of Gilbert White's *Natural History of Selbourne*

Katherine S. Anderson, 1986

Westchester County

Brinton Brook Sanctuary

Blue Mountain
Reservation

Location: Peekskill, New York
Distance: 3 miles
Owner: County of Westchester

Here is one of the places in Westchester County where stimulating walks will reward you with magnificent views. In the Blue Mountain Reservation, the prospect from Mount Spitzenberg is one of the best.

Blue Mountain is a multiple-use park. It offers a sportsmen's center for fishing, archery, and rifle practice, a bathing lake, and a picnic area. A fine trail lodge can be rented for conferences. The park's biggest asset, however, is its natural beauty.

There are usually Canada geese on the lawn next to Loundsbury Pond. As recently as the 1960s, these geese would have been a rare sight in the county except during migration. They have since become a "nuisance bird" because of their increasing numbers.

In order to understand why this has happened, you must know a little about the life-style of Canada geese. These regal birds are grazing animals, just like cows. They eat grass and prefer to graze where the grass is kept short. Lawns and golf courses are ideal. They nest on the edges of ponds, which, before developers arrived, were marshes and swamps.

The geese tend to be fairly sedentary because their goslings take a long time to grow up. Additionally, in late June and early July, the adults molt all their primary feathers, and, since the geese cannot fly for a couple of weeks while their new feathers are growing in, they must be near the water to escape from predators. The timing of this molt and the growth of their new wing feathers coincides with the growth of the goslings' first flight feathers, so the whole family becomes airborne at once.

Geese are faithful mates, and a goose family stays together for an entire year. The young of this summer will be chased away when nesting time comes next spring. Geese must be three or four years old before they can breed, which explains the occasional small flocks of geese without young.

Several solutions to the Canada geese problem have been suggested, but the only one that will work is to allow the grass to grow tall—not a very practical solution for golf courses. Trapping and removing the geese works only until they can fly again. These geese are game birds and make for a delicious meal, but very few are shot in Westchester (hunting laws apply). You just have to admire their beauty, courage, and family loyalty, and remember that their droppings are processed grass, which makes good fertilizer.

Access

From NY 9, exit at Welcher Avenue. Follow Welcher east to its end at the reservation entrance. A minimal parking fee is charged during the summer. From the entrance booth, bear left and park in the lot past the trail lodge.

Trail

Leave the geese behind, and start up the Red Trail, which begins opposite the lake. Within a few yards, bear right at the fork, go a few yards more, and bear left at the next fork. You will be on the "correct" Red Trail. Blue Mountain Reservation is noted for its magnificent rock formations of Hudson Highlands granite, and this trail will take you through or around many of them. Look for little natural rock gardens of grasses, ferns, and even natural bonsai trees in crevices. Mosses and lichens are abundant.

At its intersection with the Green Trail, bear right and stay on the Red Trail. Remain on this main road at all intersections, even bearing right past another small red-marked trail that circles a pond. This woodland pond is usually well populated with frogs and salamanders. Clumps of tussock sedge grow with their feet in the water; last year's brown leaves hang down like hair and new, bright green growth can be seen at the top. If you feel the stem of a sedge, you will find it to be triangular. The stems of reeds are round and those of grasses are round with joints.

Two shrubs predominate along the trail. One is the maple-leaved viburnum, whose name describes the shape of its leaves but not their

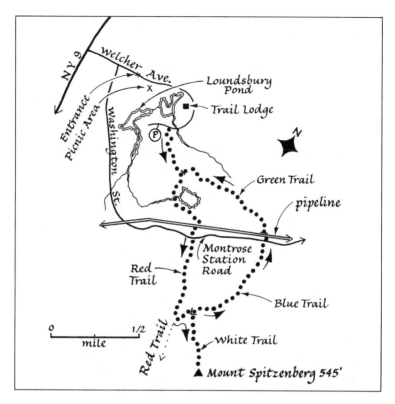

velvety softness. In June it has small clusters of tiny creamy flowers in flat heads, which will be followed by dark blue berries. It may be possible to see the tiny pink, green, and white caterpillar of the spring azure butterfly feeding at flowering time. These caterpillars are often attended by small ants that like to eat the honeydew the caterpillar exudes.

The other popular shrub along the trail is sassafras, which is actually a small tree but is seen mostly at shrub height in these woodlands. Sassafras bears three different shapes of leaves on its limbs: oval, mitten, and three-lobed glove. No other native tree or shrub exhibits such peculiar diversity in leaf shape. Income-seeking European colonists scoured the eastern woodlands for sassafras, uprooting the shrubs and sending shiploads to Europe where the plant was regarded as a cure for everything from the "French Poxe" to the plague. European settlers also smoked sassafras leaves, although a taboo existed among Native Americans against doing so. Starlike, bright green blossoms of sassafras ripen by fall into dark blue berries that are eaten by a wide variety of songbirds.

There are several riding stables in the vicinity of Blue M ntain, and the use of its trails by horses is evident. You will cross two open spaces along the Red Trail. One is a pipeline; the other is Montrose Station Road, a dirt road that traverses the park. Both of these openings provide a different habitat for animals and an "edge," an area where two habitats, such as woodland and field, meet. The edge is always the most heavily populated part of any area.

Where the Red Trail intersects the Blue Trail, turn left for a short distance and look for the White Trail on your right. After a short, steep climb of about 100 feet, this trail will take you to the top of Mount Spitzenberg.

What a view rewards the climb! You will see Haverstraw Bay and the Tappan Zee of the Hudson River with the upper Palisades on the river's west side, the Tappan Zee Bridge, and Hook Mountain, where hawks sail by in the fall. At the northernmost point of Haverstraw Bay, all the way on your right, Stony Point juts out into the water, marked at its tip by a white lighthouse. In 1779, the British fort here was captured for a short while by General "Mad Anthony" Wayne in one of the fiercest fights of the Revolution on the Hudson's shores. Imagine this view during the days of the Revolution, when the land had been cleared for firewood, industrial fuel, and charcoal; to create pastureland; and for safety reasons. You could have sat up here with a spyglass and watched the activities of British armies some distance away.

There are many options for the return trip. A pleasant way is to go back to the Blue Trail, where you'll turn right, then bear left onto the Green Trail after crossing Montrose Station Road. All trails are clearly marked.

George's Island

Location: Montrose, New York
Distance: 1 mile
Owner: County of Westchester

George's Island is a peninsula extending into the Hudson River. Natural areas, picnic areas, and river views each contribute to the park's appeal. As is true in all old estate areas of this region, many non-native plants are mixed in with naturally occurring ones. Multiflora rose and honeysuckle are two you will come upon in this park.

Access

From NY 9, exit at Montrose. Go north on NY 9A for 1.3 miles; turn left onto Dutch Street (at a large sign for George's Island). The entrance is at the end of the street. A minimal parking fee is charged on weekends and in the summer.

Trail

Leave your car in the first parking lot, to the left of the toll booth. A labeled nature trail, built by the Youth Conservation Corps in 1980, begins at the lot's south corner. (A self-guiding pamphlet is available from the park manager.) Bear right at the fork. A large white pine has dropped its cones on the path. These cones have scales that are very sensitive to dampness. By closing up when wet, white pine scales protect the winged seeds between them. On dry, breezy days when the cones open, the seeds are released. They fly to new patches of ground, where they have a better chance of sprouting than they would have had under the parent tree.

Bear right at an intersection with another trail. On both sides of this trail, sapling and mature pignut hickory trees grow; the bark on their trunks and limbs is furrowed with intricate black lines that resemble stenciling, and the leaf is actually made up of five leaflets. As you walk down the trail, you might find the fresh, green husks of the nuts in

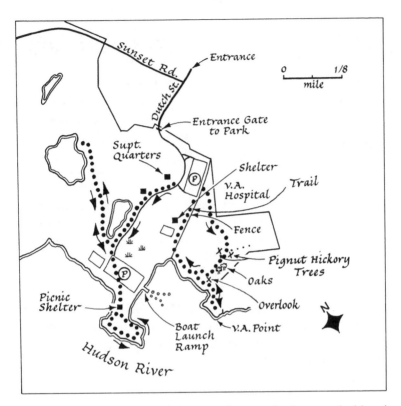

autumn or, at other times of the year, the same husks turned old and brown. The name pignut may refer to the bitterness of the nuts—fit for forest-rooting swine but not humans!

The trail leads you to your first glimpse of the river. Growing among the rocks at the overlook are some large chestnut oaks. These oaks, with their strongly furrowed bark, prefer to grow on rocky hilltops. The "chestnut" in the name refers to the tree's leaves, which look like those of the chestnut tree. Rock oak might be a better name.

The trail goes down the hill to the right. Bear left at a Y junction to go down to the river. In April look for Dutchman's-breeches and columbine among the rocks to the left of the path. This trail dead-ends at the river. Walk back up to the base of the hill, and then continue straight. Follow along the river, past the telephone cable, until the trail comes close to the Hudson, widens, and turns right to head away from the water. Follow this trail past the picnic pavilion (on your left), along the narrow paved road to the parking lot. Along the way you can compare the leaves or the leaf scars, depending on the season, of staghorn sumac and ailanthus. The leaf scars of the ailanthus are very large horseshoes, while those of the sumac completely surround the bud.

Follow the main paved road left downhill toward the river. There are beautiful willows along the way. One is the weeping willow, with long pendant branches; the other is the black willow, with more upright branches. Swans nest on a small pond to your right, and long-billed marsh wrens sing from phragmites, which are tall reeds from Asia that grow in wet areas.

Take the right at the end of the pond. This trail is overgrown along its edges and is an almost impenetrable thicket that is wonderful cover for birds and rabbits. Cottontail rabbits do not dig burrows in the ground but rest in small depressions under thick shrubs. These depressions are called forms. Rabbits are not rodents—because their incisors are different—but they use their incisors as rodents do to cut their plant food. Rabbits are prolific breeders. Their nests consist of shallow holes in the ground covered with a blanket of dry grass and fur from the female's body when she is not in attendance. The female, called a doe, visits the nest at dawn and dusk to feed her young. These little bunnies are on their own by the age of six weeks, and the doe proceeds to bear another litter. Very few of the little ones survive the hazards (predation, disease, and competition for limited resources) of their first summer of life.

Beyond the thicket the trail leads to a knoll that overlooks a large pond. In the early twentieth century the Hudson Valley was known for its brick industry. Many buildings in New York City, as well as in Westchester County, were built from bricks made at George's Island. At that time this pond was a clay pit. Now it is a freshwater pond, reputed to be 80 feet deep, and is not connected to the Hudson River. The local name for the pond is Lake Whoopee; you will see evidence of such activities around its edge. On the far side of the pond is an extensive growth of narrow-leaved cattail, where birds such as the Virginia rail like to hide. The clay for which this area was famous can be seen in the trail itself. If the path is wet, it can be slippery.

Return along the same trail. Look for thimbleweed blooming in June. This white flower will be followed by a cluster of seeds, tightly wound up with soft fibers and shaped like a thimble.

Back on the road, cross the lower parking lot and bear right toward the picnic shelter. If you look up into the shelter's roof, you will see two kinds of nests made of mud. One is the nest of the barn swallow, a dark blue and orange bird with a forked tail that feeds on flying insects. Because it builds its nest in sheltered places, a barn swallow may use the same nest year after year. Most other birds make new nests each spring.

The other mud nest is made by a mud dauber wasp and is actually a brood chamber for its young. When a mud tube or clump is complete, the female wasp provisions it with paralyzed spiders, then adds newly laid eggs and seals the chamber. The eggs hatch into larvae that feed on the spiders. They go through the pupal stage within the chambers and emerge as adult wasps in the spring. Many of these wasps are electric blue in color and may be seen collecting building material around the edges of mud puddles. They are docile insects, and there is no need to fear them.

Bear right along a path that runs on a bank above the water's edge. The Stony Point monument is visible across the river. Look out over the cove for feeding ducks. In winter loons may be seen here. The common loon, which nests on northern lakes, spends the winter along the ocean coast or in rivers like this, calmly feeding in waters so cold humans could not survive in them.

Loons are ancient birds. Their fossilized remains have been found in rocks 67 million years old. The name loon comes from a Scandinavian word meaning clumsy. The bird's legs are set so far back on its body that it cannot walk on land, but loons are accomplished swimmers. They are known to dive as deep as 240 feet below the surface of the water and to stay under for as long as three minutes.

As you walk along this path, notice signs of former human occupation. The early Native Americans left most of the oyster shells you see. During the 1920s a mansion existed here, with cabins, a tennis court, and a ball field. One of the major users of the site was the American Canoe Association. Flotillas of canoes used to paddle from Dyckman Street in Manhattan to this peninsula for outings. Westchester County purchased the land from the federal government in 1959.

Interesting plants along this path include hackberry trees, seaside goldenrod, and a very large swamp white oak. The path circles the point and returns to the parking lot.

Graff Sanctuary

Location: Croton, New York
Distance: 1.25 miles
Owner: National Audubon Society
(managed by the Saw Mill River Audubon Society)

Its proximity to and view of the Hudson River give Graff Sanctuary a special flavor. The sanctuary is also unusual because a large part of its forest consists of magnificent tall tulip trees mixed with large Norway maples. The introduced maples, along with such shrubs as molle viburnum, come from the days when there were several large landscaped estates in the area. On the other side of Furnace Dock Road is a county park called Oscawana. As yet undeveloped, it is nice to wander in.

Access

From NY 9, exit at Senasqua Road. Turn left (north) on NY 9A. Pass Sky View Nursing Home and continue for about 1 mile. Turn left onto Furnace Dock Road just before the entrance to a Daitch Shopwell supermarket. After about 0.25 mile, look for the sanctuary's entrance near the third telephone pole after a brown house on the left. The sign is set high. Roadside parking.

Trail

At the Graff Sanctuary entrance, three red dots on a rock in the wall indicate the start of the White Trail, which leads steeply down to a damp area. If there is ice underfoot, walking may be difficult. When you arrive at the foot of a bedrock outcrop cliff, watch for the white marks of the left fork of the White Trail that signal you to leave the beaten path and climb the steep hillside. From the valley floor, with its spicebush and springtime jack-in-the-pulpit, the trail goes around the base of a rocky knoll. Look up at the rock to see an unusually large example of how black birch trees grow from rock crevices. They can survive in such difficult living situations for a long time.

The top of the plateau you will reach consists of open deciduous woods. In late summer there is a ground cover of white woodland asters, each plant a delicate bouquet. Later, their empty seed receptacles will shine in the winter sun. As you start down the hill on the other side (not so steep), you will pass a linden, or basswood, tree with seven trunks of similar size, all apparently coming from one root system. This tree produces white wood valued for carving. Native Americans made rope from its tough, fibrous inner bark, which is so strong it cannot be broken by hand.

Crossing the brook below depends a little on the water's depth—you may have to look around for a series of good stepping-stones. The brook flows through a carpet of trout lilies in spring.

The White Trail bears to the left and follows the ridge above the

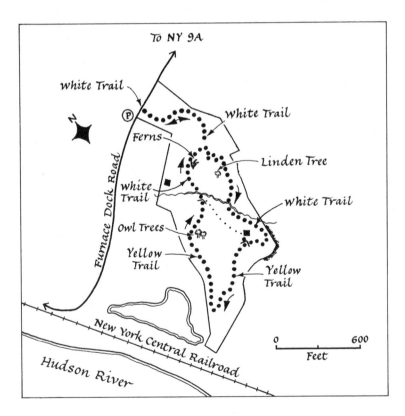

brook to a stone wall; it then curves to the right again. Continue as you sight a large stone building. This peculiar structure with stone steps to lure you to its top was apparently part of a water system for the estate on the Oscawana property. At one time there was a hole in its top, but it has since been cemented over for safety's sake. No other holes or pipes are apparent. Whatever its original purpose, the structure now provides a wonderful place to sit among the treetops and watch for birds and other animals.

Go back on the White Trail a bit, almost returning to the stone wall, and take the Yellow Trail on your right. It wanders through a small forest that primarily consists of black locust trees, which attest to the young age of this part of the woods. Black locust is one of the "pioneer" trees, among the first to colonize old fields. There is also a tangle of honeysuckle vines underfoot, which are something of a nuisance to walk through. Honeysuckle's only redeeming feature is that deer and rabbits like to eat it. If only they would eat it faster!

A line of old fence posts parallels the Yellow Trail for a while on your left, another remnant of the farming era. You will be heading toward the river—you can see it glistening through the trees and feel the wind sharpen. The sound of an occasional train reminds you that you are not far from civilization. On windy winter days you may hear ice grinding along the Hudson's eastern shore. You cannot actually get to the river from this point because of the terrain's steepness, but the views are memorable. You will also overlook a small lake (on private property) frequented by kingfishers and ospreys. The lake is less turbulent and murky than the river, so it is an easier place for these birds to fish.

The Yellow Trail bends away from the river and follows the edge of a steep descent to a gorge. If you look carefully as the trail bends to the right and starts up a small hill, you will find evidence of the great horned owls that live in this sanctuary. "Whitewash" can be seen on some of the tree trunks, and remains of owl pellets can be found on the ground. These pellets are made of hair and bone from the owls' food; they are cast from the birds' mouths but are not unpleasant to handle if they are dry. Skulls, claws, and various bones are recognizable in these pellets. The large rabbit population is doubtless one of this sanctuary's attractions for owls because rabbits are the preferred food of these fierce tigers of the air. If the crows are active, they may show you where one of the owls is roosting. Crows are also on the owls' menu, so they will harass an owl they find sleeping in the daytime.

Follow the Yellow Trail back to its intersection with the White Trail and bear left. You will pass beautiful rock formations and several small, steep-sided gorges. The White Trail bears right near some more old fence posts and passes through Christmas ferns. On the right is a rock shoulder covered with polypody ferns and partridgeberry.

Ferns have a long and complicated life cycle. Rarely are "baby" ferns seen, for they are so small they are hard to observe. Spores released from the dots on the backs of fern leaves grow into minute plants called gametophytes. Sexual parts develop within each gametophyte. When the egg and sperm unite, usually through transportation of sperm in water, a sporophyte develops. Conditions must be perfect for a sporophyte to become a mature fern; most of the billions of spores produced never complete the cycle.

The White Trail bears left just past a small, dying hemlock grove and retraces the first part of the walk back to the sanctuary entrance. If you would like to go down to the river, drive down Furnace Dock Road. It will bring you to a parking area where there used to be a train station. The bridge over the tracks here is unsafe. Continue around the curve and you will come to a pull-off area on your left, with a trail going out to a rocky shore along the river. (This is county property.) Continue on this road to Crugers Station Road and back to NY 9A, or you can retrace your route.

Brinton Brook Sanctuary

Location: Croton, New York
Distance: 1.5 miles
Owner: National Audubon Society
(managed by the Saw Mill River Audubon Society)

Willard and Laura Brinton found their homesite by walking from Peekskill and following a topographic map. When Laura Brinton donated this land to the National Audubon Society in 1957, she called it a "living museum of this region." If you are interested in birds, plants, geology, or water, there is something here for you to enjoy.

Access

From NY 9, exit at Senasqua Road. Go left (north) on NY 9A (Old Albany Post Road). After passing Sky View Nursing Home, continue 0.3 mile. Look for a sign on the right: Kenoten, Weinstein, Private Drive. Turn right here and follow the drive about 0.5 mile to the sanctuary parking lot.

Trail

From the parking lot, take the Yellow Trail to the south (through the fence to the right, not straight ahead). This trail runs along the base of a hill and is a wonderful sun trap in winter. The snarls of grapevines among the trees provide excellent cover and food for small birds and ruffed grouse. You can expect to "put up" at least one of the ruffed grouse in this area. Apparently, the grouse can control the amount of noise it makes on takeoff. Sometimes it rises with a startling, thunderous sound, and sometimes it rises in complete silence. There is a theory that some of the loud noises animals make, such as the slapping of beavers' tails or the noise generated during the takeoff of grouse, are not just for warning but

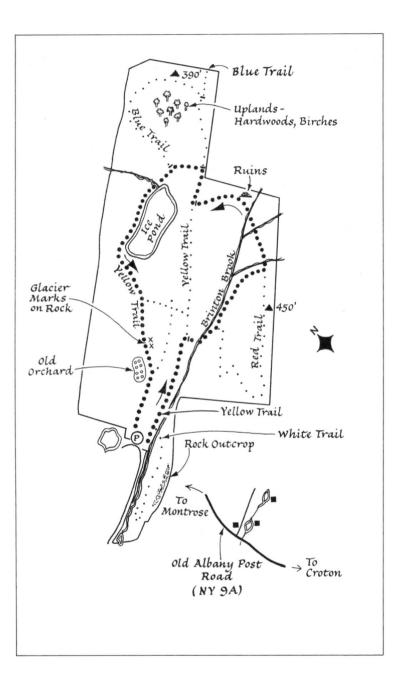

are intended to throw predators off balance by startling them, making the predators reveal their locations. It seems, though, that grouse tend to be quieter during hunting season.

Lots of deer signs can be found in this area, too. Deer are browsers, and a close look at the twigs of shrubs or low-growing maples reveals shredded ends. Deer have no teeth in the front of their upper jaws; they twist and pull twigs with their lower jaw teeth, working against a hard pad in the upper jaw. One deer is said to consume between 15 and 20 pounds of this material each day. Like cows, deer are ruminants. They graze as they walk along, and then lay somewhere in hiding to regurgitate the material and chew it, swallowing it again for complete digestion.

Turn right onto the Red Trail. Ahead is what was once a thick, dark hemlock forest. The trees have been killed by the woolly adelgid, an alien insect that sucks the sap and life out of hemlocks. It will be interesting to see what will replace the hemlocks on this site.

The brook crossing is a good place to see raccoon tracks. The Red Trail leads to one of Brinton's most appealing features—the split rock spring. A stone seat invites you to sit awhile near water bubbling from the split in a huge rock. The water temperature in the pools (which were built by Willard Brinton, an engineer and inventor) stays almost the same year-round—48°F. As a result, the pools rarely freeze, and tadpoles and frogs can sometimes be seen even in winter. In early spring egg masses of spotted salamanders are attached to twigs below the water's surface.

Continue left on the Red Trail and cross a small dam. At the next intersection turn left, still on the Red Trail. This section will take you along another hillside and past some old foundations. The story of the foundations, as told to me by Laura Brinton, is that a slave named Jesse Davis ran away from his masters before the Civil War and went to sea as a pirate ship cook. When the war was over and slaves were emancipated, Davis took his earnings and built a little subsistence farm on this spot. We don't know how long he lived here nor which of these foundations was house and which was barn. Davis probably kept this land cleared for many years. The stream you just crossed would have been his water supply.

Eventually the Red Trail meets the Yellow Trail again. Turn right onto the Yellow Trail—an old farm road, somewhat depressed, with stone walls along each side. It can be very wet in spring. Make a left onto the Yellow Trail where it meets the Blue Trail. You will pass another intersection with the Blue Trail. Slowly and quietly approach the ice pond. Great blue herons, green herons, and various ducks may be surprised there. The trail goes across the stone and earth dam that retains the pond. Five acres in extent, the pond was built as an ice source. Shortly after the pond was filled, however, someone invented the electric refrigerator, and the entrepreneur's ice business soon disappeared.

The pond contains green frogs, bullfrogs, many varieties of fish, and some of the biggest snapping turtles alive. One, seen here sunning on a rock, had a tail as thick as my wrist. Snapping turtles are omnivorous, preying on ducklings, fish, small aquatic invertebrates, carrion, and a surprisingly large amount of vegetation. Big turtles have no natural enemies; their population is mainly kept in check by raccoons and skunks, who eat turtle eggs. Turtle nests are dug in sunny spots. Sometimes twisted pieces of leathery shell can be found near a small hole—evidence of a midnight feast.

The trail continues through several open fields, which are mowed every three years with a tractor in order to keep them from reverting to forest. Summer is their most beautiful time, with clumps of orange butterfly weed, yellow black-eyed Susans, white yarrow, and a beautiful grass called Indian grass all in bloom. An annual butterfly count, conducted by the Saw Mill River Audubon Society here in July, has recorded as many as 22 different butterfly species.

On the left past the meadows is a huge rock shoulder of gneiss, smoothed and grooved by glacial action 10 thousand years ago. This is a great place to climb up and sit quietly for a while to observe the goings on in the trees and thickets across the path. In spring and summer you should hear, and I hope you will see, an indigo bunting, one of the most beautiful of all blue birds. Blue feathers do not have blue pigment. The color is structural (the feathers are actually gray) and is the result of the reflection or refraction of light rays. Find a blue jay feather; hold it up to the light and look through it. You will see that it is gray. Yet the three blue birds of this area—blue jay, indigo bunting, and bluebird—look brilliantly blue.

The trail passes through an old apple orchard, another remnant of farming days. The trees are slowly dying and falling, but those left still produce fruit. There is a pear tree, too. This is a good place to see deer and box turtles feeding on fallen fruits in the fall, and it is a good place for birds year-round. "Birds of Brinton Brook" is a published listing of 129 breeding and visitor birds available from the Saw Mill River Audubon Society. You may telephone the society at 914-666-6503. From this point, the trail goes directly back to your car.

Croton Point Park

Location: Croton, New York
Distance: 2 miles
Owner: County of Westchester

Croton Point is one of the most beautiful parks in Westchester. A visit to it provides a grand overview of the way much of the land has been desecrated yet some of the best has been saved. If this sounds contradictory, just take a look at this park. But first, check the tide tables in the daily paper; low tide is the time to go. If you would like to join a guided tour that celebrates the history and importance of this site, join Chris Letts of the Hudson River Foundation for his annual Christmas and New Year's Day walks. Call the park first to confirm the date (914-271-3293).

On your left as you approach the park is the huge landfill that was Westchester's prime dump for many years. "You could look across a marsh—it was all cattails—we used to pick the punks to use on the Fourth of July," said Tony Colao, Westchester County's northern district park director. He grew up near Croton Point and remembers when what is now the dump site "was all water and marshland, and you could see across to Ossining." Now "Dump Mountain" blocks the view. As incinerators in White Plains and Yonkers closed in the 1960s, tons of household garbage arrived every day at Croton Point. Scavenging gulls, starlings, and crows numbered in the thousands. After great controversy, the landfill was finally closed in June of 1986. Its role was filled, to some extent, by the garbage-to-electricity plant at Charles Point in Peekskill.

Dump Mountain is currently overgrown with phragmites, goldenrod, and tree saplings. There are plans to seal and cap the dump with a plastic liner and to reseed it with a grass cover. This two- to four-year project, which will require over $30 million to complete, should prevent toxic leachate from leaking into the Hudson River. While the dump is being capped, all visitors will be required to park at the gate entrance.

It is estimated that, as of 1992, every American disposes of 1,200 pounds of garbage per year; only 10 percent of this garbage is recycled. Currently, 8 to 10 percent of Westchester County's garbage is recycled. New York State's goal is to achieve a 40 percent recycling rate by the turn of the century.

Access

From NY 9, exit at Croton/Harmon. Turn west toward the railroad station. A light regulates traffic over a very narrow bridge. Go past the dump to the very end of the road and park in the far left corner of the large parking lot. A $5.50 fee is charged, if you do not have a county park pass, from Memorial Day to Labor Day.

Trail

On to the fun part of the trip. From your parked car, walk westward toward the magnificent Hudson River. On most good days you will see people fishing along the shore. The Hudson, though it has suffered mightily because of human disregard, is now making a comeback. Striped bass, shad, herring, and blue crab are increasing. It is currently unsafe to eat striped bass because of chemical residues, including polychlorinated biphenyl (PCB), in their bodies, but at least these fish can live in the river. The New York State Department of Environmental Conservation publishes guidelines for amounts of Hudson River fish and shellfish that can be safely eaten. It is available from municipalities and wherever fishing licenses are sold.

Much of the lawn area on which you are standing is fill, made in the same way as the dump behind you. Along the beach farther to the south, winter storms often tear off great chunks of soil, exposing bottles and plastic bags—old garbage that has been used to support new land.

There are several very special reasons for visiting Croton Point. One of the best is beachcombing, which is why you should go at low tide. On the new- and full-moon tides, you can actually circumambulate Croton Point, following the six to seven miles of beach. As you walk left along the grassy picnic area (a great place for kite flying), you will approach the beach, the natural Croton Point. An alluvial deposit of sand, silt, and cobbles, this beach was created over eons by the Croton River as it flowed into the Hudson, a process that continues today.

Treasures can be found at this beach. The driftwood alone would be difficult to resist if it were not lying so far from the car. There may be huge trees, some with roots still intact, polished to a silvery sheen by the water's action; there are tiny pieces of driftwood in animal shapes. Then there is the residue of past ages: broken bits of brick polished by the water, remnants of the Point's old brick-making industry; shards of china; polished colored glass; a teaspoon from a doll's tea set. You may find skeletons of fish left by fishermen or washed up dead and scavenged by the gulls. Or you might find old pilings from the Underhill Brick docks, where 100 years ago sloops and schooners moored to take on bricks. The local brick industry flourished up and down the Hudson River, using the same clay Native Americans used to create their cooking pots.

Two favorite things to search for are caltrops and clay babies.

Caltrops are seeds from the European water chestnut, an alien plant that grows under water. They are black and hard, with four points positioned in such a way that no matter how they rest on the ground, one point sticks up. During the Middle Ages, when wars were fought on horseback, metal caltrops were made and flung on the field of battle in the hope that enemy horses would step on them and become disabled. Imagine stepping on one of these in your bare feet! Though the seeds are supposed to be edible, they are almost impossible to find. The submerged stems of the water chestnut are also hazards to navigation because they can foul ship propellers.

Clay babies are unique formations made when water seeps through the banks of clay that line Croton Point (clay from which bricks were once made). When the water meets an obstruction (such as a grain of sand), precipitated lime forms odd shapes. Geologists call these shapes concretions. They are light gray in color, and they feel chalky when they are rubbed. The first clay baby is difficult to find, but after you know what they look like—and they look like everything from animals to small humans—they seem to pop out at you from the thousands of stones on the beach.

If the tide is low enough, you can walk along the beach to a small cove where a number of old side trails lead to the top of the bank. Otherwise, retrace your steps along the beach, and look for a trail going into the woods on your right where the lawn begins. Follow this trail to arrive at the camp area. The cabins here can be rented during the summer, and it is apt to be rather crowded; but from September until June you can enjoy solitary walking on land that has a long and interesting history.

The Kitchawan people lived from Croton Point north to the Hudson Highlands. The name these people gave themselves was Lenape, which translates simply as "The People." The word Kitchawan actually describes the place where The People lived—"the high bank." Their name for Croton Point was Senasqua, which contemporary speakers of the language translate as "grassy place," perhaps an allusion to the tidal marshes that once flourished here. Upon this neck of land in the mid-1600s stood a "castle" or palisaded native fort, village, and burial ground. Discovered in 1899 by Mr. Harrington of the Museum of Natural History in New York City, the earthworks of the fort were "low but well defined."

Croton Point is only one of many similar points along the Hudson River, juts of sediments where major tributaries enter the Hudson Estuary. Each and every one of these sites was heavily used by various peoples over time. Croton Point was (and still is) an especially good place for fishing and shellfish collecting. Oyster middens—piles of discarded shells—line the shore. Some of these shells are thousands of years old. Oysters no longer grow in the Hudson, probably because of siltation and salinity changes—oysters are very sensitive to both.

The Van Cortlands owned this land after the Native Americans. Perhaps the most interesting owners were the Underhill brothers, who hybridized native grapes with European strains. Prior to the early 1800s, European grapes had not grown well in this country because they could not withstand local insects and diseases. Underhill wines were reputed to be of great medicinal value and were highly recommended by doctors. The magnificent English yew trees, midway out on the point at the end of the cabin area, were planted by the Underhills, whose house stood in that area.

Croton Point's tip offers a beautiful view of the widest place in the Hudson, the Tappan Zee, spanned by the graceful bridge of that name. Tappan is pure Lenape, and translates as "a place that is cold or frosty." Zee is pure Dutch, and means sea. Tappan Zee means "sea of the Tappans" or "sea of the people who live at the cold, frosty place."

The high promontory on the right is Hook Mountain, an excellent place for hawk-watching on fall days (Croton Point is good, too). Rock formations along the western shore of the river are part of the Palisades. From the tip of Croton Point, known as Teller's Point, you can see the badly eroded trail that leads down to the Hudson. This erosion has exposed the bank: notice how it's all just a big pile of silt and sand.

As you walk back from the point, take a dirt road downhill to the right. Feel the sun pouring into this southern exposure! This is an excellent place to see birds in any season. Near the bottom of the slope, on the left, are two old Underhill wine cellars built into the side of the hill.

The shoreline on your left is overgrown by tall, plumed reeds called phragmites, an Asiatic reed that has supplanted the area's native cattails. Past the pine grove, take a turn to the right. This trail will take you down to the edge of South Cove. You will be looking at Croton Bay Estuary, the confluence of the Croton and Hudson rivers. Croton River, a major tributary that drains much of Westchester County, descends its last length through a steep-sided gorge (where you can go walking in another county-owned park) and empties into the Hudson, creating an upwelling and mixing of nutrients. Herring, striped bass, and shad use this rich estuary for spawning, and the fishing for stripers and shad is excellent. From Teller's Point, eagles are commonly seen fishing in winter, and osprey fish in late summer and fall. Mink and otter, along with raccoon, opossum, and muskrat, roam the beaches; you can look for their tracks. Within the conifer groves live resident barred and horned owls. Ducks float on the bay, an important wintering site for waterfowl.

You will have to retrace your steps from the edge of the cove back to the pine forest. Then go straight up the hill past the brick house. As you pass the dump, take a long look at this archaeologists' nightmare waiting for the year 5000. Then go home and work on your town's recycling program!

Rockefeller State Park Preserve

Location: Pocantico Hills, New York
Distance: 1.5 miles
Owner: State of New York

The Rockefeller family has always been generous in allowing public use of their lands for walking, skiing, and horseback riding. In the early 1980s, 750 acres of this property were given to the state of New York, with more to follow. Trails that were built with horses in mind make for very easy and pleasant walking when they are as well maintained as these. Markers are plastic discs nailed to the trees.

Access

From NY 9A or the Taconic State Parkway, take the exit for NY 117. Drive west 0.3 mile to a light. Turn left on NY 448. At 0.1 mile, turn right onto Old Sleepy Hollow Road. Continue 1.6 miles to the intersection with Sleepy Hollow Road. Park anywhere along Sleepy Hollow Road on the roadside. There is no entrance sign here for this park.

Trail

From your car, walk across Sleepy Hollow Road and enter the park by a metal gate. The Pocantico River flows to the left. In spring clumps of penstemon, or beardtongue, flower along the sides of the trail. It is amazing to see bees immerse themselves in these flowers to reach the nectar deep inside. The woods are dominated by tall tulip and oak trees. At any time of year you can find oak leaves from the previous autumn on the forest floor. The leaves are strong and waxy and require years to decay into soil. The oak genus, called *Quercus*, can be divided into two basic groups, both of which can be found at Rockefeller State Park Preserve. Those in the red and black oak group have leaves with pointed lobes; those in the white oak group have rounded lobes. The two groups also grow different-looking acorns. Acorns of the red and black oak take two years to grow to maturity on the branch; the insides of their shells are hairy, and the nutmeats taste bitter from high amounts of tannic acid. White oak acorns take only one year to mature; the shells are smooth inside and, although they can taste bitter, are not half so bad as the acorns of the red and black oak. Acorns from the chestnut oak, a member of the white oak group, even taste sweet and nutty.

Red-bellied woodpeckers frequent these oak trees, making their strange mewing calls. The red-bellied woodpecker is a recent emigrant from the south. It has a fluorescent red-orange banner from the top of the head down the neck, but the red on its belly is so faint it can only be seen when you are holding the bird in your hand.

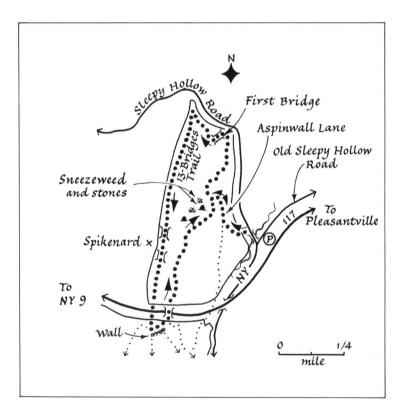

*Permits are given for people with carriage horses to drive on
the perfect trails of Rockefeller State Park.*

At a T intersection, turn right onto Aspinwall Lane. This road will
lead you to another T intersection; turn right again. You will be on the
Thirteen Bridges Trail; the blue discs on the trees bear a TB and are
numbered. Late summer is the time when flocks of winter birds form in
woodlands such as these. Chickadees, tufted titmice, white-breasted
nuthatches, and downy woodpeckers are constant companions. Flocking
behavior helps the birds find sources of food to share and also protects
individual members from predators, since all are on the alert. When
warblers pass through during fall migration, they often join resident
flocks of birds. Any flock is worth investigating for surprises.

At the first bridge you come to there is a large clump of wild ginger. An unusual wildflower, ragged robin, blooms here in June. It is pink with frayed-looking petals. Jewelweed is abundant in summer. Many of its leaves show the work of tiny caterpillars that eat the inner layer of the leaves, leaving tunnels behind. Gory Brook meanders back and forth under the trail, thus the need for thirteen bridges.

There are many large hemlocks to the left of the trail, which are good places to find roosting owls throughout the year. Several small trails branch off from the main road, but continue to follow the blue discs. You'll find clearweed growing in damp soil near each bridge. This small, shiny plant has translucent stems, which inspired its name. Clusters of tiny greenish flowers emerge from the leaf axils. Clearweed is of the nettle family but it has no stinging hairs.

Another rare wildflower grows on the right side of the trail between two bridges that are close together. This wildflower is called spikenard and is a member of the Aralia family. It has very large, double-compound leaves, spikes of small white flowers, and dark purple berries in the fall. Though it is a perennial herbaceous plant, spikenard appears shrublike.

After the trail passes under NY 117, walk up a slight grade and turn left. A stone retaining wall on the right has some clumps of evergreen ferns growing in crevices between the rocks. One is the Christmas fern, a leathery fern common throughout the woods. The other is ebony spleenwort, a small, delicate fern that requires limestone soil in order to thrive. It has wiry black stems and can be found at all seasons of the year. The small, white flowers of sweet cicely can be seen on this wall in spring, followed in summer by ribbed seeds that have a faint anise flavor if they are nibbled on while they are still green.

Turn left again, still on Thirteen Bridges Trail, and take the overpass back over NY 117. Bear left at the fork to follow the blue discs. Farther along the left side of the trail, large stones have been erected as a curb to keep you from plunging down the steep hillside. Sneezeweed blooms among these stones in summer. This yellow flower somewhat resembles the black-eyed Susan, but it has a higher center cluster of florets. Its name comes from the practice, many years ago, of drying the plant's leaves and using them as a substitute for snuff.

Many small, bright orange chanterelle mushrooms are scattered among the leaf litter in late summer. August rains and high humidity encourage the growth of many other varieties of mushrooms here. Most show the teeth marks of chipmunks or the feeding trails of slugs. The plants' gills or pores are often full of tiny insects.

Turn right onto Aspinwall Lane, then left to go back to the road and your car.

Teatown Lake Reservation

Location: Ossining, New York
Distance: 1.6 miles
Owner: Teatown Lake Reservation

One of the largest and finest nature centers in Westchester County, Teatown Lake Reservation was originally a gift from the Swope family. With smaller additions of land from other generous citizens, Teatown has grown to more than 300 acres. Several fine Tudor-style barns house a museum, its shop, and the reservation staff. There is a maple syrup house and a small collection of native animals, notably several species of owls and hawks that cannot be released because of disabling injuries.

A preserve of this size has many trails. The most popular one here is probably the two-mile walk around Teatown Lake. A much less trod area, containing the Marsh and Meadow Trail and the Hidden Valley Trail, offers more variety.

Access

From the Taconic State Parkway, take the exit for NY 134 west (toward Ossining). Turn at the second right onto Spring Valley Road. Follow this road about 1 mile. Reservation buildings and the parking lot will be on your right.

Trail

From the parking lot, meander past the sugarhouse and down toward Blinn Road on the red-marked trail. The trail parallels Blinn Road for a few hundred feet. Trees have grown around the old ribbon wire attached to them many years ago—an indication that this land was once pasture. Cross Blinn Road at the sign for Marsh and Meadow Trail, and wind your way along the edge of a swamp and up onto a rocky promontory.

Skeletal cedar trees grow on top of the rocks here; only one has a few green branches. These trees tell of once open land in decades past, since cedars grow in bright sunlight. Now the cedars are overshaded by black birch and maples. Just before the trail descends a small hill, notice the green stems of catbrier along the trail on the right. This thorny plant can make impenetrable thickets, offering fine winter protection to rabbits and birds. It sometimes bears blue fruit, which is edible by animals, and its new leaves in spring can be eaten by humans, too.

Go through a stone wall to emerge in the meadow: You'll pass first through a marshy patch of rushes, sedges, and sensitive ferns beside a boardwalk, then into a mowed area that is a wave of goldenrod in summer. Note the healthy, symmetrical red cedars growing in the full sunlight. If this field were not mowed but left to its own, deciduous seedlings would sprout, grow, and eventually overtop the cedars and turn them into skeletons—just like the ones you saw on the rocky outcrop in the woods. Turn left onto the red-marked trail where a sign directs you to Hidden Valley. There are two young trees standing alongside this trail. These black walnut trees are offspring of the large trees along the wall that divides the meadows. Take a close look in springtime at their fuzzy, pointed buds. The tree's large leaf scars look like monkey faces.

Over the next wall you will enter an area that is rapidly becoming a complete snarl of vines punctuated by a few white spruces. The vines include grapevines with peeling brown bark, bittersweet with orange berries, and honeysuckle with black berries. The honeysuckle retains some bronze-and-green leaves in winter. Both bittersweet and honey-suckle twine tightly around sapling trees and strangle them. Their virtue lies in their food value for wildlife: berries for birds and browse for deer.

Follow the trail to the right and enter a beautiful, fragrant white pine grove. This grove has been nicely maintained, as you can see by the dead branches that have been pruned and piled. You can guess the age of the trees by counting the whorls of branches and adding five for the first year of a tree's growth. These trees appear to be about 50 years old and were planted to form this plantation. Wild trees, of course, need no pruning to survive.

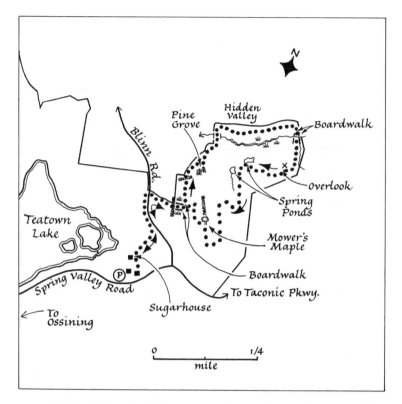

Head back into the deciduous woods and down a short slope. Turn left at the T intersection, cross the bridge, and bear right at the foot of the cliffs. Some of the tall, straight trees beside the path are tulip trees, others are ash, yet others are hickory. A few on the right are—incredibly—tall, straight sassafras trees. Occasionally, the usually shrublike sassafras attains tree size. The root of this tree/bush was once used in spring as a tonic and thinner of the winter blood. Recently, however, sassafras has been found to be carcinogenic when taken in very large doses.

The sun pours into the side of the valley. In spring you can actually look up the slope into the faces of numerous red trilliums. Small springs trickle down the slope to feed the swamp and brook. As you walk the base of the slope, notice the piles of angular rocks—talus—formed by frost action that heaves apart the cliff's bedrock.

Hemlocks soon appear. In spring you'll find an abundance of skunk cabbage, false hellebore, and marsh marigolds in the swamp on your right. In winter spectacular ice formations decorate the many small caves and crannies in the rocks.

Keep your nose alert, too—sometimes you can smell a fox! Foxes have musk glands that give off an odor similar to that of skunks but that is more delicate and not long-lasting. Foxes can control this odor. They seem to delight in releasing it when they are watching you, knowing full well that you will never see them.

The trail turns sharply to the right over a boardwalk. Along the brook at the end of the walk is a large stand of wild leek and, in season, many clumps of hepatica. The leek sends its leaves up in early spring, looking much like the leaves of lily of the valley. In July these leaves have all died down; then the naked stalks of white, starlike flowers appear, to be followed by shiny black seeds.

You will climb a very steep hill beside a rushing brook. Standing among hemlocks at the top, you can look back over the trail you have covered. The trail leads you through a dense stand of mountain laurel, one of America's most spectacular shrubs and known not only for its glossy leaves and spectacular flowers but also for its convoluted trunks and brown bark. In colonial days the hard wood of the mountain laurel was whittled into various utensils, giving the shrub the name "spoon wood." Mountain laurel buds look like decorations for a fancy cake, and its wide-open flowers have a unique beauty. Many flowers are specialized in some way to encourage pollination by insects. Laurel flowers have stamens caught at their tips within depressions in each petal. When a bee lands on a flower cup to reach for the sweet nectar in its center, the insect's weight releases these stamens and pollen is sprinkled onto the bee's back. The pollen is then carried to another flower, and thus seed production begins. You can use your finger as the "bee weight" to see this happen. Laurel is evergreen; the thick stands that are found in the area's woodlands provide good winter cover for birds and deer.

Continue on the red-marked trail through more laurel to the Spring Ponds Trail, which will take you past several ponds. The ponds are called vernal ponds because they are usually full of water in spring but dry up in summer. Actually, these ponds are usually full of water in fall and winter as well. They are active breeding ponds for spring peepers, wood frogs, toads, and salamanders. The second pond also contains a wood-duck house, which is occupied each year.

Bear left, keeping on the red-marked trail. This path winds around and down back toward the meadow. At the T intersection with the old country lane, turn right. Standing in the wall separating the two meadows is the largest tree at Teatown. This huge sugar maple has been dubbed the Mower's Maple because men mowing these fields by hand may have rested in its shade 200 years ago. Retrace your steps to Blinn Road and back to the main building. The museum and the gift shop, which has various books, hand lenses, and other nature-related items, are open all day Tuesday through Saturday and on Sunday afternoons.

Kitchawan Preserve

Location: Ossining, New York
Distance: 1.5 miles
Owner: Westchester County

Kitchawan is derived from the Lenape or Delaware Indian word Kichamonk, which means "great hill," "truly a hill," or "high bank." Kichawonk refers to the people who lived in that place, "the high-bank people," which might refer to the banks of either the Croton or Hudson rivers nearby.

Access

From the Taconic State Parkway, exit at NY 134. Go east 1.5 miles. The preserve's entrance is on the left. Parking is available.

Trail

Before the buildings, take the dirt road on the left past a wooden gate. Turn right at the sign for Little Brook Nature Trail, which is marked in yellow. The trail is called a labeled nature trail because it is the work of an Eagle Scout. His labeling has now fallen into disrepair except for a few fern and tree names. One large sign on the left discusses the characteristics and demise of the American chestnut, the former glory of the northeastern woods. Most of the old, weathered stumps seen in these woodlands are chestnut stumps. They can be recognized by their gray color and by the vertical striation of their wood. The stumps often support beautiful lichen and moss colonies.

When these trees died of a fungus imported from China, local residents quickly cut them for building material and fence posts. Some of that fencing still exists. Research on the chestnut fungus continues in the hope that a control will be found before the sprouts that still come up from the trees' old roots are lost.

Little Brook appears to be a young brook—the sides of its bed are very steep and no floodplain has developed. The brook flows to the Croton Reservoir, which borders the preserve.

The presence of many reservoirs in Westchester affects the use of the area's ponds, lakes, and rivers. Any pond or lake that empties into a reservoir is under the control of both the State and the City of New York. If you wish to put chemicals into a pond to control algae or fish, or for any other reason, you must receive permission from both the city and state.

Study the different textures of tree bark as you walk. Each tree species has its own unique pattern of bark growth. White ash has a precise diamond pattern, which is not to be confused with the more irregular corrugations on the tall, straight tulip trees. Black birch has horizontal lines, called lenticels, on black bark with some vertical cracking. Sugar maple is the gray-trunked tree with the rough bark that develops into deep clefts with age. The ghostly, pale gray bark of beech seems smooth as skin. The trunk of ironwood looks like a smooth, gray, muscled arm. Only red maple exhibits a variety—sometimes scaly gray with smooth patches, sometimes all smooth, sometimes with some cracks.

Some of the most visible animal traces along these trails are mole tunnels, many with holes where the animals must have emerged for nightly forays. Moles do not hibernate. They spend the winter below the frost line, tunneling for earthworms—their primary food source—and for other burrowing creatures such as the grubs of May and Japanese beetles.

Moles have the most beautiful fur of any mammal. (Don't the kings in fairy stories sometimes wear capes of moleskin?) One characteristic of this fantastic fur reflects the animal's burrowing life-style. Unlike other mammal fur, which stands on end if stroked backward, the mole's velvety fur lies flat no matter which way it is stroked. If, as a mole tunnels along, it comes to a large rock or root it cannot get around, it must back up. But the tunnel is the same size as its body. If its fur stood on end when it backed up, it would constantly be full of dirt.

Another animal that may make itself known to you in these woods is the ruffed grouse or partridge. When alarmed, these large birds take off with a thunder of wings. The ruffed grouse is the area's woodland chicken, spending most of its time on the ground in search of food. It usually roosts on the ground or low in thickets. As winter approaches, the grouse grows small bristly feathers along its toes, providing it with winter snowshoes. Its tracks in snow can be identified by its almost toe-to-heel print. If the ground is snow covered and food among the leaves is hard to find, grouse will eat buds from shrubs and trees.

In fall or spring, when you hear a sound like a distant motorcycle engine trying in vain to start, you may be hearing the drumming of a male grouse. The bird stands on a log and fans the air with his wings so quickly that a drumming sound is produced; but he does not actually hit the log with his wings. The sound assumes the function of song in other birds, serving to identify a territory and to attract a mate. It's very difficult to see a grouse drumming, but the bird may be closer to you than you think.

At the T intersection, turn left onto the green-marked trail. You will soon come to a sign for the Beech Grove. Turn left onto this brown-marked trail. There are many individual beeches in Westchester woods, but beech is the dominant tree in this spot. Note how abundant the young ones are, each waiting for a chance to replace a parent tree. Not many trees in the forest can grow in shade this way.

The trail through the beech grove continues onto the watershed property and eventually to Croton Reservoir. This land is not open to the public, so you must glimpse the reservoir through trees; then turn around and return to the sign directing you up the Red Oak Trail to Jackson Hill.

Some of the roots, rocks, and logs along this trail sport beautiful growths of a moss called delicate fern moss because its leaves resemble ferns. It has taken at least 50 years for moss to cover these rocks, so be careful not to disturb it. Moss adds organic material to thin soils and is of great value as a ground cover and in preparing the soil for future, more "advanced" plant growth.

Look for deer prints in muddy places. The hemlock grove along the ridge to your right provides good shelter for deer. Where the trail snakes around a few bends and begins to approach the hemlocks on the slope, maidenhair fern grows on the right among the Christmas ferns.

The Red Oak Trail gradually follows the slope of Jackson Hill. Red oaks have bark with long, vertical ski-trail stripes that are flattened and shiny. At the top of the hill you will see a place where some wood has been cut. The drive for alternative energy sources makes it necessary for woodland owners to keep a sharp eye out for wood rustlers.

Follow the wide truck path to the next intersection. A left turn here will take you back toward your car.

Turkey Mountain Park

Location: Yorktown, New York
Distance: 2.5 miles
Owner: Town of Yorktown

Turkey Mountain was preserved through the efforts of concerned citizens who recognized its value. Though the park's problems—principally vandalism and fires—are still many, the appeal of its woodpeckers, bluebirds, impressive rock formations, and beautiful views far outweigh them. The wily wild turkey, reintroduced into the northern section of the Hudson Valley by the New York State Department of Environmental Conservation, has wandered back into this park that bears its name. Watch for fallen feathers, and listen for the gobbling of the male, most often heard in spring.

Access

From the intersection of NY 202, NY 35, and NY 118 in the center of Yorktown Heights, go south on NY 118 for 2 miles. Look for the park's entrance sign on the right just beyond the high-tower power line. People driving north on NY 118 from its intersection with NY 129 will find the entrance on their left. Parking is available.

Trail

Leave your car in the parking lot, and don't be in a rush to get to "the top." There is a lot to see at lower elevations. From the parking area go straight on the Red Trail, past a metal barrier. After entering the oak and maple woods, the trail climbs up on some rocks. Admire the huge boulders with their miniature gardens of moss, blueberry, and partridgeberry. Among the rocks bloom lovely lady's slippers and native orchids more beautiful than expensive hothouse varieties (please don't pick them). Some of these massive boulders sport a growth of rock tripe, an edible lichen that has a faint mushroom flavor. Perhaps in an emergency it might taste good (if you like to chew old leather). Of course, don't even dream of picking these rock tripe to try out their taste. As a result of increasing air pollution, these once-abundant, spectacular large lichens have all but disappeared. Those that survive here have spent decades, perhaps even centuries, growing.

The old foundations you will see in the park are leftovers from the 1930s when this was a summer camp. Follow the Red Trail to these remains; bear right and then left onto the White Trail. The path goes through moist woods and over a small stream. The common shrub of this area is spicebush, whose red, shiny berries are a prime food for robins and

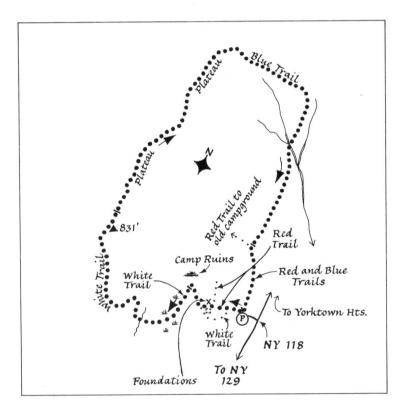

other thrushes during migration. Ferns of several varieties decorate the forest floor.

There are many worm castings in the moist soil of the trail near the brook. Worms are vital to the creation of soil. They are active at night, pulling decaying leaves and other plant matter into their holes, eating it, and releasing many of the plants' minerals into the soil. At the same time, they create air spaces in the soil (even plant roots need air) and tunnels that rain can go into, helping the water soak in rather than run off.

Small trees that have fallen across the trail have formed natural dams that hold the soil as it washes down the trail and help keep it out of the stream. The same principle has been used by people who build "check-dams" on the steep parts of the trail.

Listen for drumming woodpeckers. Woodpeckers use drumming to define their nesting territories and to attract mates. The more resonant the hollow tree, the louder the noise. Anyone who has heard a woodpecker drumming on a house's drainpipe will appreciate their staying in the woods. Woodpeckers often make holes in houses, too. The most recent theory to explain this is that the birds hear tiny sounds made by electrical wiring within house walls and think the sounds are insects. Woodpeckers have very sensitive ears, and they locate wood-boring insects by hearing them.

It soon becomes apparent that most people who use Turkey Mountain are on their way to the top. This White Trail is very well packed, and alignment of parts of it have been altered to take advantage of rocks and to eliminate erosion. When you stop to catch your breath, be sure to turn and look back. The views along the way are lovely, and you will be impressed by how high you already are.

The view from the summit (831 feet) is spectacular: the Croton Reservoir and Dam, the Hudson River, Maryknoll's Oriental towers, and New York City's skyline far in the distance. If you know your mountains, you can pick out the South Gate of the Hudson Highlands, off toward the right, with Manitou Mountain on the east bank, Dunderberg Mountain on the west, and Bear Mountain looming in between. This is a good place to sit and look for hawks. Bluebirds nest here, along with field sparrows and prairie warblers. The summit's plants show the effects of the area's high winds, the proximity of bedrock to the soil surface, and the low soil moisture; they are mostly stunted and twisted into interesting shapes. Some of them, such as the little scrub oaks, cannot be found at lower elevations. There are many deerberry shrubs, which do not have edible fruit, and blueberry bushes. Clumps of pale corydalis huddle in rock crevices.

As you begin to follow the Blue Trail, you will see evidence that fire has been a way of life to this mountain. Today forest management includes the use of fire to keep ground material from building to such depths that a fire would kill even the biggest trees. Fires that burn quickly take the underbrush but leave big trees alive. New plants invade after a fire—grasses, wildflowers, blackberries. The animals that have been able to flee and survive benefit from this new growth.

The Blue Trail goes eastward along the ridge, where different views present themselves. Much of the area is open and grassy, and there are more interesting plants such as the bastard toadflax, a parasite that lives on the roots of other plants. There are two turns to make—just remember to take the right-hand turn at each opportunity. If you come out under a power line, you have missed one turn. There is a very steep descent on this trail, so watch your footing. It helps to place your feet sideways against the slope, to keep from pitching forward.

Many wonderful rock formations border this trail. As the ancient glaciers scoured the top of the mountain smooth, they broke rocks from the south side and left them in giant rock piles. The call of the pileated woodpecker echoes from these cliffs, a dramatic setting for the Northeast's most dramatic woodpecker.

The Blue Trail, a community service project, was laid out and built by the first Walkabout class, an alternative high school in Yorktown. It is considerably longer than the White Trail and affords a chance to enjoy the lower slopes of the mountain. Where the Blue Trail meets the Red Trail, a right-hand turn wanders around the old camp area; a left-hand turn will take you back to the parking lot.

Choate
Sanctuary

Location: Chappaqua, New York
Distance: 0.75 mile
Owner: Saw Mill River Audubon Society

You can see deer, fox, weasel, and many different birds in this 28-acre sanctuary, even though the traffic noises from NY 133 are ever present. Choate is an unexpected little oasis amid the suburbanization of Chappaqua.

Access

From the Saw Mill River Parkway, take the NY 133/Mt. Kisco exit. Turn right at the end of the ramp, then left to go west on NY 133 (Millwood Road) 0.5 mile to Crow Hill Road on the right, opposite the Presbyterian church. The sanctuary sign is 100 feet farther north on Crow Hill Road. Do not park on this road—use the church lot.

Trail

Use care in crossing busy NY 133 from the church lot. Notice the marsh on your left that is full of sweet flag, not cattails (no brown, cigar-shaped seed heads can be seen); the sweet flag flower is down low among the leaves. Follow Crow Hill Road for about 100 feet. The sanctuary entrance is on the left.

Enter a typical bottomland woodland of red maple and spicebush. On your left is an aging colony of gray-stemmed dogwood (*Cornus racemosa*) shaded by the surrounding trees. Their branches stretch for sunlight. Be alert in fall for flocks of birds feeding on the shrubs' white berries, which are highly favored by migrants.

Just before the bridge, briefly leave the main trail by going straight ahead over a stone wall and bearing right into a small meadow. This is the only open land in the sanctuary, except for the marsh at the corner of NY 133 and Crow Hill Road. This meadow has bushes of honey-suckle, multiflora rose, dogwood, blueberry, maleberry, and saplings of cherry and other trees growing in it. These shrubs are cut every so often to allow what once was a herbaceous meadow to naturally change into a shrubby meadow.

Return through the wall to the main trail, turn right, and walk over a small bridge above a stream. This stream originates in a pond off the property and runs all year. Tracks of raccoons are usually evident. Winter wrens frequent the stream's brushy edges in cold weather.

The moss that covers the rocks you see here has taken at least 50 years, and perhaps more, to grow—a long life for such a seemingly insignificant life form. Jewelweed is abundant beside the bridge in summer and fall. Hummingbirds almost always appear at clumps of jewelweed during fall migration.

At one time, there were many large, dead spicebushes along this trail. Spicebushes throughout the region were infected by a fungus disease and died in large numbers. The Carey Arboretum of the New York Botanical Garden was consulted, and they suggested cutting and burning all infected plants. Audubon Society caretakers believed the recommendation was not only undesirable but also impossible, so the cure was left to nature. The spicebushes have since resprouted. This is a good example of how ecosystems are able to manage themselves successfully.

Cicadas will be trilling on hot summer days. Annual cicadas, which spend just one year underground as nymphs, take six weeks in the sun to reproduce. Then they die. Every 17 years a different kind of cicada may appear. The 17-year cicada is black and orange and slightly smaller than the brown and green annual drummer; its call is much quieter and sounds like a distant generator. The incredible sounds that both cicadas emit are made by tympanums, or drumheads of skin, on the sides of their muscularly vibrated abdomens. It is the males who "call." People sometimes refer to these insects as locusts, but the real locust is a kind of grasshopper well known for the damage it can do to crops, especially in dry areas.

Go through the second wall, turn right, and at the next intersection bear right. Christmas fern forms a dark evergreen boundary to the path. Bear left at the Y. On your right, about 20 feet into the woods, sit small piles of cobbles. These are rock piles heaped by farmers clearing their fields for planting and are different from the natural weathering that produces the fall of rocks upon the slope, which you can see beyond the farmers' rock piles.

It's a green, green world—but the shades of green are so variable! Where the trail bends left, you can see two forms of very different greens on the right—Christmas fern and marginal shield fern, one dark and glossy, the other almost turquoise and matte-finished. By the trail on the left is a growth of yellow-green grass, probably one of the plants the deer enjoy eating here.

Go up the hill and through another wall. Look in the wall on the left for the skeletal cedar, an indication that this tree once grew in the full sunlight of a farmer's old field. Most of the large trees in this sanctuary

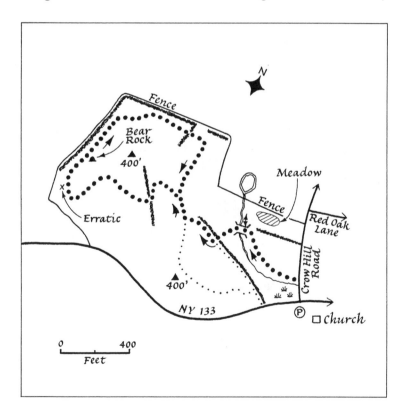

are oaks. During gypsy moth infestations they are apt to be leafless in July; their recovery during off years is apparent.

As you go over the crest of this hill, you will be constantly aware of the noise from NY 133. Go downhill again, passing New York fern that is a bright yellow-green. Its leaflets taper at both ends of the stem. Snakeroot usually blooms here in early summer, next to a long log on the ground. Look carefully at this point to see an interesting association of insects. Aphids have their beaks in the stem of the plant, and ants cluster around them. The ants guard the aphids from predators and benefit by drinking the "honeydew" they exude from their abdomens. Some ants will even take these aphids into their underground homes for winter protection.

You will approach a huge erratic—a boulder that stands alone, dropped here by a glacier—that makes a dramatic contribution to the landscape. Along the right side of this trail as it winds down between two ridges, one rock looks to me like a bear's head. Do you believe rocks have spirits? Three times I photographed this bear's head rock, and three times the film came out blank.

Up a little hill, and down again, and you will see another small rock pile on your right. Many dead trees stand in the woods, mostly black birches phased out by the maturing deciduous canopy of sugar maple and oak. These standing dead trees are important sources of food and nesting sites for woodpeckers. What would happen to the woodpeckers if there were no dead trees left standing? Everyone with a wood-burning stove should know which trees to take and why to leave some dead wood standing.

Walking quietly pays off. If you walk with friends, try to talk later so you can observe nature. Once, while I was quietly looking up a pretty plant called spreading dogbane in my wildflower guide, a cabbage butterfly came gliding along and lit on a dogbane flower. All of a sudden the butterfly began flapping madly without going anywhere. Close examination showed that an ambush bug had driven its sharp stiletto right between the butterfly's green eyes. Suddenly there was a buzzing, and a white-faced hornet proceeded to grab the prize away from the ambush bug. Carrying it up to a low tree branch, the hornet cut off the butterfly's wings, rolled up the rest, and then flew off with it, probably to a nest to feed some hungry hornet larva. It was an incredible performance, seen only because I had been still.

The trail may become obscure; just follow the white markers. Notice the sparse-needled red cedars as you walk. There are only a few, yet these sickly individuals are large for their species. Off to the left on a down-slope, one huge red oak with dead lower limbs dominates the woodland. Notice how these lower limbs curve out and then up, an indication that this aging red oak originally grew in the full sunlight of an open field. Later the red cedars sprouted, followed by deciduous saplings that overtopped the cedars and took their sunlight, changing the field into forest.

Bear left at a Y in the trail, then left again, to go back to the sanctuary entrance. If you continue straight, you will be on the sanctuary's second loop. Marked by yellow dots, it has some spectacular cliffs and is slightly shorter than the walk just described.

Pruyn Sanctuary

Location: Chappaqua, New York
Distance: 1.5 miles
Owner: Saw Mill River Audubon Society

Pruyn Sanctuary supports a small herd of deer on 60 acres of lowland and ridge, swamp, and beautiful rock formations. This is an excellent place for birding, especially during migration. Over a 10-year period of banding birds with federal leg bands, more than 90 species have been encountered here. You can see all the woodpeckers to be found in this part of the country: downy, hairy, flicker, red-bellied, and pileated.

Access

From the Saw Mill River Parkway, exit at NY 133, Mt. Kisco. Go west on NY 133 for 2 miles to a stoplight at Seven Bridges Road. Continue on NY 133 for 1 mile to Woodmill Road on the left. The sanctuary is off a stub road on the right near the end of Woodmill. Roadside parking.

Trail

Leave your car on the road, but be careful not to block any driveways. After you have walked a short distance into the sanctuary, you will see a bulletin board on the right. This walk is only one of several to be made at Pruyn Sanctuary. A map is available in the nearby registry box.

Walk straight ahead along the bed of an abandoned road and past a typical mixed deciduous wood of black birch, sugar maple, and gray birch along with towering oaks and beech. Off to your right, downhill of the roadbed, is an ash and red maple bottomland swamp with a well-developed shrub layer of spicebush and American holly. At the end of this old road, turn right onto a boardwalk. You will be on the Green Trail. Where the boardwalk takes a left turn, a slow approach to the pond's edge straight ahead may result in your seeing a wood duck, mallard, or spotted sandpiper. Many birds can be found in this swampy area year-round.

What is the difference between a swamp and a marsh? A swamp has trees while a marsh has none. This swamp boasts a magnificent growth of skunk cabbage in spring. Tussock sedges, royal ferns, and marsh marigolds follow in season. This pond was human-made, but it is not very successful. The brook that feeds it has a low flow gradient. As a result, siltation is rapid, and most of the pond on this side is a mud flat in summer. Where the boardwalk parallels the brook, you will see the remains of a dike built to keep the brook out of the pond. Periodic high water and tunneling by muskrats have made this dike impossible to maintain. Maintenance of this area, historically used to bottle drinking water, is being discussed. Current plans are to turn the mud flat into a small pond.

There is a bridge over a brook at the T intersection. You can cross over to get a better look at the pond and to visit the bird blind, then return to continue on the boardwalk. In summer the cinnamon ferns resemble a tropical jungle, and swamp azaleas fill the air with their perfume.

At the end of the boardwalk, sphagnum moss grows over the hillocky rhizome mounds of cinnamon fern. At Stake 11, just beyond the end of the boardwalk, grows a young chestnut tree. At one time, American chestnut was the dominant tree of these woodlands, blooming across the landscape in late spring and ripening a vast crop of chestnuts each fall. In 1904 an Asiatic fungus disease destroyed the chestnut trees. From time to time, however, a sapling chestnut can be found suckering up from older roots. These saplings never attain any great size; they succumb to the disease while still quite young. The boardwalk continues again after a short distance on the ground.

Dead trees are evident all along these trails. According to sanctuary policy, dead wood is left alone, except when it is moved off the trails. That is why so many woodpeckers come here. The red-bellied wood-pecker is one of the newest birds to invade this region from the south, and it is staying year-round. Thirty years ago the area's largest wood-pecker, the pileated, was rarely seen in Westchester. Now maturing forest

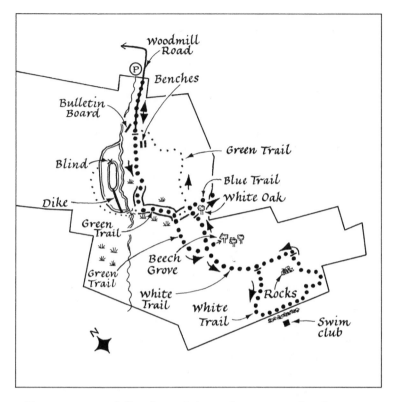

with carpenter ant–infested trees is increasing, encouraging the presence of this crow-sized bird.

Where the boardwalk makes a sharp left-hand turn, bear right onto planks, still on the Green Trail. Notice the dewberry, a blackberry that creeps along the ground, growing over the sphagnum moss. It has three shiny leaves on a slender green stem protected by thorns.

At the Y intersection, bear right onto the White Trail, which leads through a beautiful beech grove to a higher area. Spring beauties carpet the forest in April. Take the white-with-red–dot trail branching off to the right. As recently as the mid-1980s, this area was a young forest with occasional stumps and logs of long-dead American chestnut. Those signs of the chestnut trees are now gone. The trail soon bears left and parallels a stone wall with a swamp on the other side. The path along the wall catches an extra-thick leaf fall, and walking it is like walking on a mattress. Rocks in the wall are beautiful, covered with lichen.

Much of the sanctuary consists of deciduous woods. The word deciduous comes from the Latin word *caducus*, meaning "inclined to fall" or "transitory." The shortening days of autumn are key to the dropping of leaves. Short days mean that the trees, using the energy of the sun, water, and nutrients from the soil combined with the green chlorophyll in their leaves, can no longer manufacture food. The green pigment then breaks down, and the reds, yellows, and other pigments that were masked by that green become visible.

When sap ceases to flow from stem to leaf, a sealing-off layer of cork, called the abcission layer, is formed, and eventually the leaf drops to the ground. Trees such as beeches and oaks, which retain their leaves much of the winter, have only partial abcission layers. Their old leaves sometimes hang on until they are pushed off by the new growth in spring.

Most of the leaves that drop have at least small holes in them. The energy created by the tree serves to feed a great many small creatures, including aphids, caterpillars, and leaf hoppers. Once the leaves reach the ground, they are slowly consumed by other herbivores, among which are worms, springtails, and sow bugs.

The trail winds up into the deciduous slope community of sugar maple, black birch, tulip tree, and ash, past some rock formations. If you lose sight of the trail itself, simply follow the paint markers. Turn left when you reach a wider path, and go back to the start of the White Trail. Just before meeting the Green Trail again, look at the bark of a large white oak on your right for bark beetles. These cousins of fireflies are evident in the bark crevices on all but the coldest days of winter.

Turn right onto the Green Trail, then bear right onto the Blue Trail at a four-way intersection. This trail leads through a very moist valley where unusually fine wildflower displays can be seen. Sometimes deer can be spotted on the tops of the hills above this ravine. One of the things they seem to enjoy eating in April is the flower of the Dutchman's-breeches, whose rejected leaves are abundant here.

There are several kinds of vines up this slope: grapevine, honey-suckle, woodbine, and, unfortunately, Oriental bittersweet, which must be constantly battled. Along the top of the slope are plants, such as jack-in-the-pulpit and spicebush, that are normally found in lower terrain with more moist conditions. There must be water under there somewhere! Down-slope again, past spring carpets of Canada mayflower and ever-green Christmas fern, there is a large patch of wild leek on the right. Its leaves, which resemble lily of the valley, come up in early spring. In June they die, to be followed in July by naked flower stalks with typical onion flowers and shiny black seeds. In the south this commonly eaten plant is known as ramps. The leaves are quite tasty used raw in salads or as an ingredient in leek soup.

The Blue Trail takes you back near your point of entry. Turn right.

Pinecliff Sanctuary

Location: Chappaqua, New York
Distance: 0.5 mile
Owner: Saw Mill River Audubon Society

Saw Mill River Audubon Society is privileged to own several small sanctuaries, mostly in the Chappaqua area, that serve a special function as protected wetlands. Pinecliff Sanctuary is one of these. Wetlands are very important to maintaining underground water tables and soaking up excessive rainwater. While this Audubon sanctuary is small (approximately seven acres), it is important because it adjoins larger green spaces and provides a variety of habitats for several interesting groups of animals.

Access

Pinecliff Sanctuary is at the end of Pinecliff Road, off NY 120. Pinecliff Road is the third street on the left beyond the Quaker Meeting House, or the third street on the right after the Saw Mill River Parkway overpass in the village center. Park on the roadside.

Trail

The entrance path leads right, between two ponds, one open and one almost a swamp with many trees. The open pond sports an incredible variety of water life, especially insects and amphibians. If you want to investigate these creatures, take a kitchen strainer and two small (preferably white) pans with you. Put some water in the pan, then scoop with the strainer, trying to get muck from the pond's bottom. Dump the muck into one pan and sort through it. Put anything that moves into the clear water of the other pan. You may find toad, frog, and salamander tadpoles (salamander tadpoles can be identified because they have external gills and legs from a very early stage). The nymphs of dragonflies and

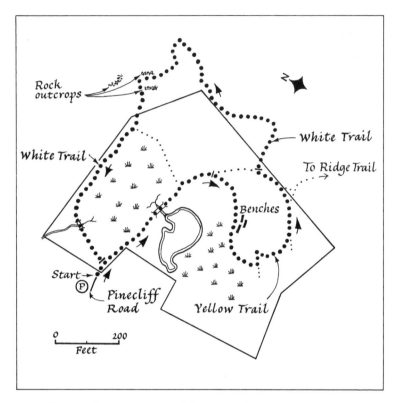

damselflies, and the larva and adult stages of giant water beetles, water scorpions, and back swimmers, will probably be found. When you are finished, be sure to replace the contents of both pans, muck included, into the pond. Pond muck and water teem with microscopic life forms that deserve to continue living in their habitat.

The unusual wealth of this pond results from its lack of fish. The pond's insects and amphibians have few predators. Several years ago there were many goldfish, but they have disappeared. Sometimes people who tire of watching goldfish swim around in a bowl will release them into such ponds. But goldfish, who are not native to this country, are really fancy carp. They are bottom feeders and tend to keep a pond riled up and muddy, cutting down on the oxygen supply for other life forms. If you tire of your goldfish, give them to someone else. Don't release them in a local pond.

Most of the open pond's surface is covered by a green film. This is not algae but a tiny flowering plant called duckweed. Two kinds of duckweed, *Lemna* and *Wolffia,* can be seen. Duckweed is the world's smallest flowering plant, though its flowers are rarely seen because the plant reproduces by vegetative division. In the hand they feel and look like green sand. Duckweed is the favorite food of the beautiful wood duck. A pair frequents this area in spring, the female shielding her ducklings in the tangled vegetation of the swampy pond. Wood ducks nest in hollow trees, and a number of dead trees with old woodpecker holes that are ideal for these ducks rise from the swampy pond and the back of the open pond. Green herons and kingfishers also visit the open pond.

Just beyond the ponds, keep straight at the trail intersection, and continue until you see four yellow dots on a tree to your right. Turn right onto the Yellow Trail. After a short walk through the woodland you will come upon a mossy overlook of the swampy back of the open pond.

This overlook provides a pleasant vantage point amid the mosses and ferns for observing activity at the back of the pond and around its dead trees. Great crested flycatchers frequent this area in spring, probably nesting in one of the tree holes. The male bird calls with a raucous "Weep!" sound. Mosses here are emerald, and ferns are green and feathery. One of Westchester's less common plants, the whorled wood aster, is abundant here, too. Check your wildflower book for its leaf structure, and you will easily recognize it.

The Yellow Trail continues along the edge of the swamp, then swings to the left up the hill. It turns to the right through some rock outcroppings and will lead you down through a cluster of large beech trees to intersect the entrance trail. Make a left here; continue straight and watch carefully for the White Trail, which branches off to your right.

One of the most elusive of the area's amphibians is the spring peeper, a tiny tree frog about one inch long. Its shrill voice in early spring, when it is in the pond for mating, can be deafening. Spotting a peeper is a challenge, even though there are many in this woodland. On almost any moist day, a tiny creature may hop away from your feet. Look quickly—it matches the leaves—and you'll see a peeper. Peepers do not stray far from their breeding grounds in summer.

Follow the White Trail over a small hillock and into a little valley; bear left, then right up the hillock on the other side. A fine stand of bugbane grows there, holding its white candles of flowers aloft in late June. Like many members of the buttercup family, bugbane flowers have no petals. The flowers are clusters of stamens that have a fluffy appearance. Bugbane has other names, including black cohosh and black snakeroot. The reason it is called bugbane is a mystery, because "bugs" seem to love its flowers. The scent of these white spikes is certainly not very pleasant for people. Their form, however, pleases the eye, and the seed pods that follow are very handsome, round, and brown and persist far into the winter.

As the White Trail tops the hill, there are handsome formations of gneiss rock on your left. These rocks, folded and squished together, look like a lot of gray whipped cream. They provide interesting nooks and crannies for nesting chipmunks.

The White Trail continues down the hill and proceeds along the back of the swampy pond. Turn right to skirt the wetland. On your right grows a large, golden-curly-barked yellow birch with an interesting sculpture of roots that was formed when the sapling grew over what most likely was a dead log. The log, which has since decayed, forced the birch's roots to hump into the air. There is a cultivated species along this trail—a huge patch of pachysandra. This ubiquitous suburbia ground cover probably got its start from some strands dumped by a gardener, and the rich woodland soil and moist conditions have encouraged it to flourish. Trilliums, jack-in-the-pulpits, and ferns poke their way through the pachysandra in spring.

The trail continues past large tulip trees. Cross an outlet on a bridge, and you will find yourself back at your car.

Note: The East Hudson Parkway Authority owns much of the land east of this sanctuary. The Ridge Trail, which runs along their land, is very interesting—if you wish to walk for a longer distance, it is perhaps a mile to Roaring Brook Road and another mile back. Spring flowers such as ginger, blue cohosh, and trillium are especially rewarding on that trail.

Muscoot
Farm Park

Location: Somers, New York
Distance: 2.5 miles
Owner: County of Westchester

I n May the edges of the first Muscoot road you walk on are so full of birds you will not want to move along. Yellow warblers, barn swallows, house wrens, and orioles all frequent the shrubs and trees here. Many birdhouses have been erected and bluebirds are nearly always visible. This sanctuary's almost 800 acres encompass a turn-of-the-century farm complete with cows, pigs, chickens, goats, and sheep. Add woodlands and wetlands to that, and you have a variety of habitats unique to Westchester County.

Access

From I-684 or Saw Mill River Parkway, exit at Cross River/Katonah. Follow NY 35 west to its intersection with NY 100. Turn left (south) and drive 1 mile to the park's entrance on the right. Parking.

Trail

Begin your walk all the way to the rear of the parking area. Follow a dirt road past the cow barn to the cow pastures. In addition to birds, you may see box turtles crossing from one field to another. At the end of the cow pastures, the road forks. Bear left; you will be on the Blue Trail.

At the next four-way intersection, in about 100 feet, keep straight on the Yellow Trail through the woods. This old farm road, bordered on both sides by handsome stone walls, passes the end of a pond that is becoming very swampy, with red maples and wetland shrubs growing on the hummocks. One warm May morning while I was walking this section I heard a soft mewling sound and splashing in the water. I quietly watched the edge of the pond, and a fawn appeared, wandering uncer-

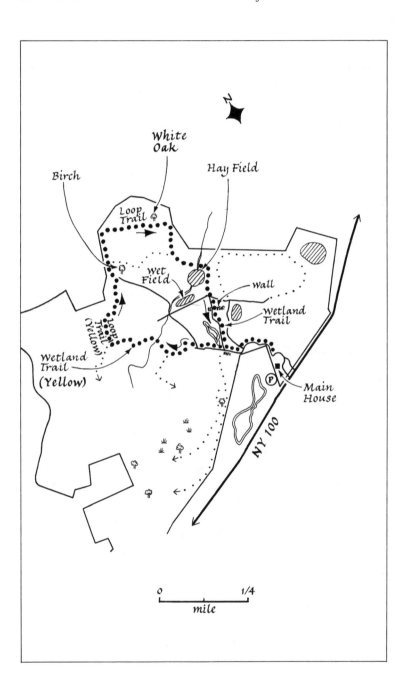

Birch

White
Oak

Hay Field

Loop
Trail

Wet
Field

wall

Wetland
Trail

Loop
Trail
(Yellow)

Wetland
Trail
(Yellow)

Main
House

NY 100

N

0   1/4
mile

tainly in the water. Then I realized its mother was there, too, feeding on water plants. The doe soon spotted me and, tail high in the air, ran off, leaving her fawn behind in the water. When I later returned to this spot, the fawn was gone. The instinct of the fawn to hide when its mother leaves is deeply ingrained and keeps it safe.

Continue straight into the woods. Notice how the bird population changes. Ovenbirds, wood thrushes, veeries, and towhees are heard, if not always seen. Both veeries and ovenbirds nest on the ground. When you see one of these birds suddenly fly up before you, spend a few minutes looking under the edges of small shrubs and ground cover. This is almost the only way to find one of their hidden nests. The Breeding Bird Atlas of the State of New York, a five-year cooperative study conducted by the Federated Bird Clubs of New York, the National Audubon Society, and the New York State Department of Environmental Conservation, indicates that as many as 64 species of birds nest in this park.

Continue straight on the Yellow Trail. Hay-scented ferns are abundant on the left. These light yellow-green ferns are covered with silvery fuzz, and they have a pleasant smell when they are crushed.

Continue through the woodland past hemlocks. After climbing a small hill, turn right onto the Blue Trail. This trail will cross a small stream where the woodland contains much black birch. In May you will see thousands of tiny black birch seedlings along the sides of this trail. They can grow in very difficult places, such as rock crevices. The trail travels over many hillocks, through small valleys, and past dramatic rock outcrops. Within the mixed deciduous woodland you may spot large, old sugar maple, oak, and tulip trees that once grew in the farmer's fields. Climb up another small hill, where the soil turns drier. One of the principal low shrubs along this portion of the trail is huckleberry. In spring you can separate it from lowbush blueberry by the golden resin dots on the back of its leaves and, when the fruit is present, by its black berries. The huckleberry has many more and larger seeds than the blueberry.

At the end of the Blue Trail, turn right onto the Yellow Trail once again. After you pass through a wall at a small swamp, continue about 100 feet and look for a pointed rock on the right. You'll find a beautiful garden of maidenhair fern, bugbane, and two of the tick trefoils: the naked-flowered tick trefoil, so called because the flowers grow on a stalk without leaves, and the pointed-leaved tick trefoil, with the flower stalk rising from the center of the leaf whorl. This trail will lead you through an area that was lumbered during the early 1980s. The increased light level has made the area perfect for such plants as blackberries. Yellow star grass blooms on the trail in spring.

As the Yellow Trail approaches an open field, look to your right for an unusual black birch with very low, spreading branches. Turn right, still on the Yellow Trail. By a large black birch tree on the left is a patch of wood betony, also called lousewort. Wort is an old English word meaning plant. Many plants were named for the properties they were thought to have. In the case of lousewort, it was thought that if sheep ate the plant they would not have lice.

One unusually large tree along this trail—a white oak—must have been standing when the wall was built 200 years ago. Muscoot Farm Park is one of the best places to see white-tailed deer because their population is large and the human invasion of their woodlands is small. Deer have browsed many of the shrubs and herbaceous plants, including the many clumps of Christmas fern in winter.

The rushing water you hear down the hill is the Muscoot River. According to speakers of the language, Muscoot is derived from the Lenape Indian word *manaskooting*, which translates as "grass cut, fallen down"; or perhaps it comes from the word *musket*, which means "swamp." Muscoot, therefore, might mean "by the swamp" or "at the swamp." Notice the sturdy, flat-topped stone wall. This wall denotes New York City watershed property. Built by professional Italian stonemasons, these stone walls have lasted far longer than the farmer's stone walls. Across the beautiful Muscoot River and up the opposite bank lies another county-owned property called Lasdon Park, which contains 227 acres of woodland, fields, and trails, with access from NY 35. Perhaps a trail will be developed to link the two.

The Yellow Trail emerges into a hay field. Keep along the left edge of this field, then cross over a stream and keep straight. The wet field to your right beyond the crossing is very interesting. Plants such as swamp saxifrage and golden ragwort (a plant with ragged-looking leaves) flower here in spring, and blue flag can be found along the edge of the stream. Later in the summer wild bergamot, or bee balm, colors the field with lavender. Keep along the left edge of the field to another stone-wall crossing and into yet another field. Follow the right edge of the field uphill, curving right, through a hedgerow. Join the dirt road, taking the right fork, which is really straight ahead. Either continue on this dirt road or watch for a right turn that will take you to the edge of the pond. There are many painted turtles in this pond; sometimes as many as 50 little heads stick up out of the water. Green herons nest nearby, and red-winged blackbirds will complain about your presence. Both yellow-throated and white-eyed vireos nest in the trees near the water; brown thrashers and prairie warblers sing in the hillside field to the left and above the pond.

The dirt road will lead you back to the farm. There is a lot to see around Muscoot's buildings, with special events that relate to farm life offered weekly on a year-round basis.

Eugene and Agnes Meyer Nature Preserve

Location: Mt. Kisco, New York
Distance: 1.5 miles
Owner: The Nature Conservancy

The Meyer Nature Preserve offers a great variety of habitat within its borders—deciduous forest, pine groves, rocky cliffs, ravines, and fields. You can find flowers, mosses, trees, and birds to enjoy in every season.

Access

Exit I-684 at Armonk. On NY 22, go north 0.6 mile past the stoplight to a blinking light. Turn left onto Cox Avenue. Bear right at a Y intersection onto Byram Lake Road. At 1.8 miles turn left onto Oregon Road. Drive uphill 0.1 mile to a small parking area on the right.

Trail

Follow the trail at the left corner of the parking area. Where a bridge crosses a stream, marsh marigolds raise their golden flowers in early spring. By July many of the spring flowers have completely disappeared, leaves and all.

You can sign in and pick up a map at the registry box. Continue along the Blue Trail. Deer flies will probably accompany you during the summer months. These very pretty flies, with patterned black-and-white wings and golden eyes, can give an unpleasant stab with their stiletto mouths, and they like to get into people's hair. The larvae of these flies live in the water, so you will often meet them where trails parallel streams and swamps.

Walk on the Blue Trail through hemlock and mixed deciduous

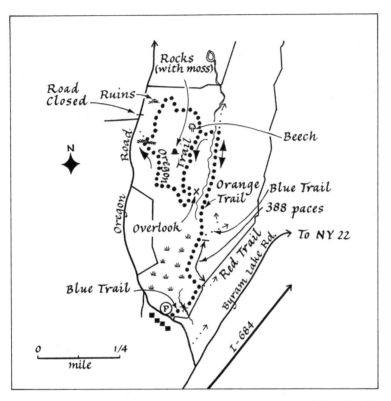

forest, and bear left onto the Orange Trail. Watch carefully for this obscure left turn across a muddy, intermittent stream and over a jut of bedrock. The turn occurs where the swamp ends on your left. If you find yourself climbing away from the swamp, then you missed the turn. As of this revision, the Orange Trail turnoff was 388 paces along the Blue Trail, if you start counting at the Red Trail junction.

White violets are spattered along both sides of this path, flowering in early spring and keeping their heart-shaped leaves all summer. The stream beside the trail rushes at times of high water, but in summer it gurgles along from pool to pool. The loud calls of the Louisiana water thrushes, who conceal their nests in the overhanging roots and rocks, echo down the ravine. In cold weather, winter wrens search for food among fallen logs in this stream, stretching their tiny legs to their fullest to observe intruders.

Turn left across the brook onto the Yellow Trail (also known as the Oregon Trail). You will see ginger and broad beech fern blooming among the rocks in May. Halfway up the hill, turn left at the T intersection. Sunlight dances off spiderwebs in small clearings; leafrollers—small, green, translucent caterpillars—can be found on the sweet pepperbush and witch hazel in spring.

Look among the many rock outcroppings for cushions of moss. The rounded, pale green mounds are aptly called pincushion moss. Sometimes chipmunks tear them apart to get soft material for lining their nests. The Yellow Trail goes through open deciduous woodland, over a series of low ridges, and into valleys. The trail turns left for a short walk to an overlook. With all the trees in full leaf, there is not much to see in summer. Unfortunately, however, there is much to hear because at this point you will be standing high above I-684.

Continue up and over ridges and across little valleys. You will pass through a stone wall, where a trail to the left continues to Oregon Road

Tall trees and distant views are part of Meyer's charm.

(permanently closed to automobile traffic) and beyond the road to large fields and pine and spruce woods that are part of this sanctuary. Continue on the Yellow Trail, turning right.

Summer is a very quiet time for birds. Even in the early mornings there is little song. Robins and cardinals, which raise more than one brood of young, still sing even into August, but most other species' young are on their own. Because the adults are going through a post-breeding molt and are no longer defending nest territories, they do not sing. This makes them more difficult to spot, especially in leafy woods.

The trail passes through a fragrant pine-and-spruce grove and into an area that was once an estate. Wall ruins, a chimney, and cultivated plants, such as privet, forsythia, myrtle, and Norway maples, are all that remain. The house, barns, and possibly a greenhouse were all destroyed by fire in the 1940s.

The Yellow Trail continues back to the T intersection, where a left turn will return you to the Orange Trail. Turn right and go back the way you came.

Arthur W. Butler Memorial Sanctuary

Location: Mt. Kisco, New York
Distance: 3 miles
Owner: The Nature Conservancy

Ridges, ravines, huge glacial boulders, and a cattail-phragmites marsh where birds come to drink and bathe all await you at Butler Sanctuary. A special area, high above I-684 and complete with bleachers, is a noted hawk-watching place during fall migration. Wood lilies raise their orange cups near these bleachers in late June.

Access

From I-684, take Exit 4, Mt. Kisco. Go north 0.25 mile on NY 172 (toward Mt. Kisco). Turn left onto Chestnut Ridge Road. Follow this road 1.2 miles to the entrance on the right. Parking.

Trail

From the parking area, walk past the entrance sign along the Red Trail. Look for the Orange Trail and turn right. In a small, overgrown field to the left of the path, a large pinxter azalea blooms in May. Thick carpets of haircap moss border the trail. Most of the other shrubs here are highbush blueberry.

The Orange Trail continues into a deciduous woodland. A huge ash beside the trail has an unusual shape. Perhaps the weight of a dead tree once lay against its branch; by the time the dead tree decayed, the branch was permanently deformed. Other peculiar shapes in trees are caused when the leader, or foremost-growing tip of a tree, is broken. Side branches then alter their directions of growth in an effort to replace the leader, resulting in interesting convolutions of the tree's trunk. These convolutions are especially noticeable in some of the tulip trees along this trail. Tulip is a very soft wood, easily broken in storms.

The Orange Trail runs along the base of a hill rising on the left, with a swamp on the right. There is a mix of ferns along the way. Where the trail enters a small field, turn right, still on the Orange Trail. You will approach a small marsh after a short distance, where you'll always find bird activity. Most birds like to bathe, and bathing keeps their fragile feathers in good condition. In addition, birds host various parasites, including feather lice, mites, and a hideous-looking flat fly called a hipoboscid; bathing helps them control these parasites. Humans only encounter these creatures when they handle birds, as they do during banding, and, fortunately, none of them are parasitic on mammals. Some birds, such as grouse and pheasants, will dust bathe to rid themselves of their fellow travelers. You may see these dust-bathing places in open areas of the trail.

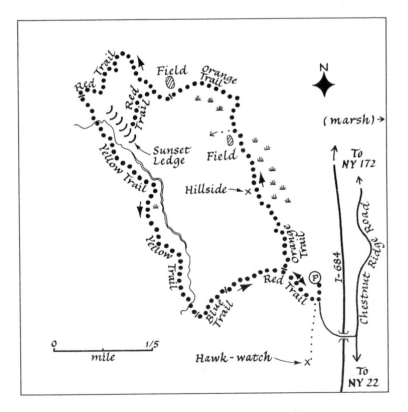

The Orange Trail turns left to circle behind a marsh where you will see cattails and phragmites. There are several poison sumac shrubs on the edge of this marsh and many clumps of red maples. Sensitive fern grows to enormous size here. As the trail approaches a large field, there are some interesting tulip trees on the left.

This meadow is ever changing. Indigo buntings sing from the tops of the red cedars in spring, when the whorled loosestrife is in bloom. Goldenrods and stiff asters bloom in September when grasshoppers and crickets are in chorus. Several clumps of bayberry can be found near the middle and end of this section of the trail.

Wood Lily

From the field, turn right onto the Red Trail. There is soon another trail to the left, an extension of the Red Trail; it is also marked in red. This side trail dead-ends on Sunset Ledge, a lovely place to sit and eat your lunch, with views to the west any time of the day. A clump of one of the more unusual milkweeds, four-leaved milkweed, blooms there in May.

Go back to the Red Trail and turn left. You may see what look like bluebird nesting boxes nailed to the sides of trees in many places throughout the sanctuary. These are actually flying squirrel denning boxes. Every day gray and red squirrels, and the ground squirrel called the chipmunk, can be seen because they are diurnal, but few people realize just how common flying squirrels are. These nocturnal creatures are seldom seen; yet they live throughout the woodlands and in our backyards. A study of flying squirrels conducted at Butler from 1977 to 1983 found 41 squirrels living on 15 acres of woodland within 50 active dens. These squirrels were live-trapped and fitted with radio-collars to track their movements. It was confirmed that the social structure of flying squirrels is quite unusual. Most male mammals aggressively carve out and defend breeding territories. Among flying squirrels, however, it is the female who does this, defending her territory against other females, but only if she is breeding. Males and nonbreeding females live together communally. A female will not ovulate until she leaves her community and establishes a territory of her own. Each female needs several tree cavities in which to raise her young because, as the babies grow, so do the fleas that eventually infest the nest. When the nest becomes infested, the young are moved to a clean cavity, until that nest, too, becomes infested. The flying squirrel population was found to vary directly with the production of acorns.

At the junction, turn left onto the Yellow Trail. You will enter an area with many fascinating boulders strewn about. The boulders make good denning areas for raccoons and foxes. You can take a guess as to who lives where by looking for scats, the droppings of wild animals. Raccoon scats often contain seeds from grape and bittersweet; skunk scats may be made up almost entirely of the exoskeletons of beetles and yellow jackets; fox scats, usually formed of fur with bits of broken bones, have a twist at the end; deer droppings look like black jellybeans. Scat observation may offend some people, but it is often the best way to determine the kinds of animals that share a woodland.

Many of the large rocks in the ravine you will enter have beautiful growths of polypody fern on them. The soil that supports this lush growth is very thin and can be peeled away from the rock like a rug. Damp and cool, this area includes a little brook that runs near the trail. At the Blue Trail, turn left. The trail rises to the top of a ridge, where it intersects the Red Trail once again. Bear right onto the Red Trail, and walk through fragrant groves of white pine and Norway spruce back to your car.

Westmoreland Sanctuary

Location: Mt. Kisco, New York
Distance: 2.5 miles
Owner: Westmoreland Sanctuary, Inc.

Westmoreland's handsome museum was originally a church, built in 1782. In 1950 the church was dismantled and stored in a barn. Much of the material in the museum, which was reconstructed in 1973, is from the church. Hand-hewn beams support the interior. The exhibit cases, made from barn siding, are in keeping with the architecture. They contain examples of local fauna, from fish to deer, as well as interesting artifacts found on sanctuary land. Educational programs on seasonal topics run year-round at the museum, maple sugar house, and outdoor lecture area. The sanctuary encompasses 625 acres and has much to explore.

Access

From I-684, take Exit 4, Mt. Kisco. Go north 0.25 mile on NY 172 (toward Mt. Kisco). Turn left onto Chestnut Ridge Road. Follow this road 1.3 miles to the sanctuary entrance and parking area on the left.

Trail

Start your walk on the Easy Loop Trail, to the right of the building. This trail will take you to Bechtel Lake. Take the Chickadee Trail toward the dam. Standing on poles in the water at the far end of the lake are two kinds of birdhouses. The tall metal cylinders are intended for wood ducks. While metal may become hotter than wood on sunny days, it protects the ducks from predation by raccoons who cannot climb metal. The houses' location alone cannot protect the birds because raccoons are good swimmers.

The smaller wooden boxes are occupied by tree swallows. These handsome birds, with bluish backs and white bellies, constantly swoop over the water to catch insects on the wing. Their nests are made of grasses and feathers. White feathers from other birds are highly favored, and the birds must sometimes fly long distances to find them. Young swallows differ from other songbirds in that they can fly well at the time they leave the nest. Robins and other such birds spend their first few nest-free days on the ground. If these fledglings were to flutter out into the water from their nests, they would not survive (except, of course, for ducks). Young swallows may not efficiently feed themselves for a few days, but the parent birds continue to provide.

Continue on the Chickadee Trail, and take the next right turn. There is a large patch of red trillium at this intersection. Turn left in a few steps onto the Veery Trail. All the trails in this sanctuary are marked by yellow plastic squares on the trees, but intersection signs will guide you. The Veery Trail parallels the outlet brook from the lake. Some of the trail goes through an evergreen forest. One of the smaller of these evergreens is red spruce. In its preferred mountain home, red spruce is an important lumber tree. Here in the lowlands, however, it is rather scrubby. You can recognize red spruce by a gall that grows on its twigs. Galls—swellings caused by insects—are plant specific. The aphids that cause the swelling on these red spruce trees live on no other plant. New galls are green; old, unoccupied galls are brown and covered with minute holes where the aphids have emerged.

Look for water striders in sunny spots along the brook. Their shadows are easier to see than the insects themselves. Each of the insects' legs makes a dimple in the water surface. If you watch the shadows, you can see how the striders "swim" on the water: the middle pair of legs propels the bug, the hind pair steers, and the front pair is held up, ready to capture another insect as food. The bugs must stay in motion here to keep from being washed downstream.

Turn left onto Fox Run Trail. As you climb a short hill, look on the left for a large, dead white oak with five trunks, one of which has fallen. Just beyond this tree there is some shinleaf, which blooms in late June and early July. Its waxy, white, drooping flowers have a sweet smell that is worth getting on your knees for. The leaves of the plant are evergreen.

Stay on the yellow-marked trail, uphill and past cliffs to a right turn onto Sentry Ridge Trail. Keep a sharp lookout for one of the most uncommon ferns of the area, the rattlesnake fern. Its feathery triangular leaves have a fertile stalk rising from their apex. This fern grows singly rather than in clumps.

On the left of the trail are some unusually large, very white quartz boulders. The trail then tops out along the edge of a high ridge. When the leaves have fallen, you will have a panoramic view of the countryside, and you can almost see down the chimney of a house below. Listen for the ringing call of the hooded warbler in May. This handsome little bird, with its bright yellow face and black hood, nests close to the ground but sings its song high in the trees.

The trail then makes a long descent to turn left to the edge of Lost Pond, where you will find a bench on which you can sit to observe the antics of the dragonflies in July. One of the large ones, the white-tailed dragonfly, patrols a territory over the pond. Each male has a favorite perch to which he returns, and, from it, he will chase any other male that flies nearby. The females have brown bodies and are welcomed into the males' territories.

Follow the trail around the pond and turn right, still on the Lost Pond Trail. At the next intersection, turn left onto Chickadee Trail. At this point you will be close to the base of some of the more spectacular rock formations in the sanctuary. Columbine, ferns, and grasses grow from crevices. There are small, intriguing caves, and the convolutions of the rocks are quite beautiful. The surfaces of these granitic-gneiss rocks are mostly weathered, but where you first come upon them, some of the overhangs have been protected from the weather and show their lines of pink feldspar. The gray, green, and powder-blue blotches covering the rocks are actually alive. These are crustose lichens.

The Chickadee Trail will return you to the end of Bechtel Lake. Walk up the hill and take the second right turn to get back to the museum.

Ramsey Hunt Sanctuary

Location: Cross River, New York
Distance: 2.5 miles
Owner: National Audubon Society
(managed by the Bedford Audubon Society)

Almost entirely wooded, Ramsey Hunt Sanctuary contains a great variety of trees, including beech groves and oak-hickory woods. The sanctuary also offers an interesting swamp walk, with numerous little bridges.

Access

From I-684, exit at NY 35, marked "Cross River/Katonah." Go east (toward Cross River) 1.9 miles. Turn left onto North Salem Road. Continue 0.8 mile to a small parking area on the road's left side, before you come to the sanctuary's sign.

Trail

Follow the White Trail, which starts at the parking area's back right corner. The trail first goes through a young forest of mostly sugar maples. Vines that climb these trees, including grape, poison ivy, and woodbine, offer good fall food for migrating birds. Large flocks of robins and rusty blackbirds frequent this cafeteria in mid-October. As the trail turns left to pass through a stone wall, the stone wall on your left becomes massive, spanning 12 feet and standing 4 feet high.

The only open area in this sanctuary is the telephone underground cable corridor. This corridor provides the edge so well liked by birds and small mammals. Continue on the White Trail, and you will pass an intersection with the Yellow Trail. Take the left fork where the White Trail divides. After passing more fine stone walls (although not as gigantic as the massive one you first saw), the woodland is shrouded with

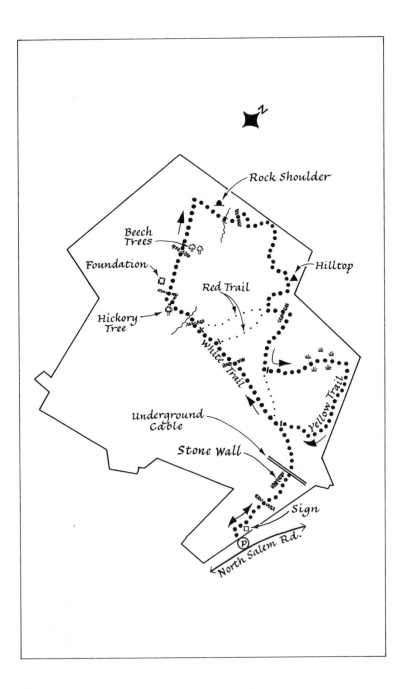

bittersweet. This vine, imported from the Far East many years ago, is an aggressive climber and will strangle many of these trees. The American bittersweet, uncommon in the lower part of New York State, is not so aggressive. You can tell the two apart—the Oriental vine has clusters of berries in each leaf axil; the American has berries at the ends of its branches. Before fire in the forest was so rigidly controlled, these vines would probably have been kept in check by occasional fire outbreaks.

Pass both ends of the Red Trail. Small bridges rise over a stream, where green frogs sit on mosses and rocks. Follow the trail through two walls, the second of which has a large hickory tree in attendance, and turn sharply to the right. On the left is an old foundation. The sizes of some of the stones in these old walls and foundations are impressive, considering that they were moved by men and oxen or horses, not by modern mechanized monsters.

This section of the White Trail passes through a beautiful beech forest. From the light green of unfolding leaves in spring to their glowing yellows and browns in the fall, beeches seem to exude sunlight. The trail makes another sharp right and descends to a stream with a bridge. To the left you can glimpse a massive shoulder of rock. Beechdrops, the parasite of beech tree roots, grow here. Pinesap, another fascinating plant that has no chlorophyll, grows near the far end of the bridge. This plant is not a parasite but a saprophyte, which takes its nourishment from decaying material in the soil. In late summer the pinesap comes up a pale yellow color; in October the stems that bear its ripening seeds are rose-pink.

Beyond the bridge you will climb a steep slope. In the summer months Ramsey Hunt is well populated with a special spider called a *Micrathena*, which likes to build its orb webs directly across paths. In this densely wooded area the clearing provided by this path may serve as a

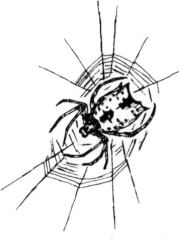

White Micrathena

flyway for insects. Sometimes the anchor lines of these orb webs that extend to surrounding vegetation can be 10 or more feet long. The *Micrathena* spiders, of which there are several species, have spiny, hard, shiny abdomens that are triangular in shape. As they hang in the middle of the webs, the spiders appear top-heavy. They are harmless, so if you walk into a web, you will only suffer a faintly unpleasant sensation of webbing on your skin. (Try not to be your group's leader!)

At the top of the hill the path bears left to a rocky overlook. Masses of mayapple bloom here in the spring. As the trail descends again look for deer tongue grasses along the right side. These grasses have very wide blades that turn yellow and brown in the fall.

At a T intersection, turn left, still on the White Trail. About 50 feet beyond an opening in a wall, the White Trail makes a sharp right. The apparent trail to the left goes to a private house, as do several others around the edges of this sanctuary. You will soon discover if you have made an error and you will have to turn around. The White Trail will lead you over another rock outcropping, where you may put up a ruffed grouse. Walk down a long slope and, at the bottom, turn left onto the Yellow Trail.

The Yellow Trail winds through a swamp, where cinnamon ferns are abundant. Their spore-bearing stalks, separate from the leaf fronds, are the color of cinnamon in spring; the fronds turn cinnamon in fall as well. The area's deciduous holly, the winterberry or Christmas berry, is common in swampy areas, with bright red fruits that hang on far into winter. It is thought that some of these fruits only become palatable to birds after they have been frozen.

As you leave the swamp the trail turns sharply right. An old fallen tree demonstrates what foresters call the "pillow and cradle" effect. The tree's uprooted base makes a pillow, and the hole makes the cradle.

The Yellow Trail takes you through good deer habitat and once more back to the White Trail. You may be suddenly startled by a loud snort—the warning a deer gives so other deer in the area will be aware of human intrusion. Deer are not known to attack people, even during rutting season when the bucks' tempers are short. But the loud snort is scary to hear.

Turn left onto the White Trail. It will lead you back to the parking area.

Marian Yarrow
Nature Preserve

Location: Cross River, New York
Distance: 1 mile
Owner: The Nature Conservancy. This sanctuary
is part of the Indian Brook Assemblage.

The Indian Brook Assemblage, which is owned by the Nature Conservancy, maintains three sanctuaries in the Cross River area. While they are not large, they provide refuges for mammals and birds that thrive in woodlands rather than in suburban surroundings. Fine specimen trees, a lake, and a pretty waterfall await you in the Marian Yarrow Nature Preserve.

Access

From I-684, exit at NY 35, marked "Cross River/Katonah." Go east (toward Cross River) for 1 mile. You will pass Mt. Holly Road on your left. Continue on NY 35 another mile, to a left turn onto that same Mt. Holly Road. At 0.2 mile bear right at a Y intersection. Continue 1.2 miles to a 90-degree left-hand turn. Drive 0.8 mile to the sanctuary sign on top of a hill. A small parking area is on the right.

Trail

Walk from the parking area straight ahead on a wide trail. Maps can be picked up at a shelter a short way in. Notice the huge sugar maples on the left. Large trees standing in a younger woodland evoke memories of former farms, as do the many stone walls meandering through this area. Most of the young trees surrounding these giants are their offspring. Sugar maple seedlings can grow in the shade, waiting for a chance to replace their elders. Very few ground cover plants grow in this dense shade.

Turn right at the Hidden Lake Loop sign. Then continue straight on this green-marked trail at a sign bearing the adage, "Let no one say,

and to your shame, that all was beauty here before you came." A common shrub here is cork-bark euonymus, a horticultural escapee. It is especially noticeable in fall after the sugar maple, red maple, and oak leaves have fallen, leaving the euonymus still cloaked in yellow and orange.

The trail crosses a small meadow, where you'll see several large red cedar trees—good places to look for cedar waxwings during the fall. Waxwings are very fond of the trees' small blue cones. In summer many grasshoppers live in this field, hatching as nymphs from eggs laid in the soil. Each time the grasshoppers molt their exoskeletons, their wing pads grow a little. By the time late summer arrives, they are flying. The males "sing" during daylight hours—some species rub their hind legs together and some rub their legs against their wing covers. Grasshopper ears are located on the abdomen.

Cross the meadow and continue on the Hidden Lake Loop. Eastern wood peewees can be heard singing far into the summer, their plaintive "pee-o-wee" coming from the treetops. These birds are flycatchers, and they like to sit on dead branches high in the trees, flying out and back on their forages for insects.

Two more small signs direct you to the lake on the green-marked trail. In any woodland where black birch is an important component, small pieces of rotting wood that are turquoise blue in color can be found on the ground. These are pieces of black birch that contain a fungus called *Chlorosplenium*. Occasionally you will see its fruiting bodies, which look like little cups.

Turn left onto the blue-marked Bass Trail. A small marsh surrounds an inlet stream to the lake. In spring the skunk cabbage here is stiff and glossy; by August it is bent, browning, and full of holes where slugs have enjoyed their evening meals. This trail parallels the lakeshore, and you will find small clumps of monkey flower along the lake's edge. Yellow markings on the lower lip of the lavender flower may resemble a monkey's face.

Turn right at the end of the Bass Trail. In summer floating duck-weed on the lake is pushed by breezes into ribbons and swirls of varying shades of green. The reflected trees look like part of a tapestry in the open water. Swamp milkweed blooms in July near the overflow culvert, and you may see orange and black aphids on its stems. Almost all insects that feed on any kind of milkweed have this coloration, which serves as a warning to birds that the insects taste bad because they have ingested the glycosides that milkweeds contain.

Pickerel frogs, with large squarish spots on their backs, hunt insects in the damp grass. They make prodigious leaps to reach the water. Green frogs bask along the shoreline, giving loud squeaks as they jump from under your feet.

Just past the culvert, turn sharply left onto the Falls Loop Trail,

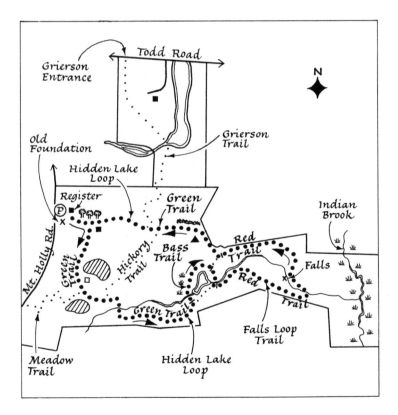

which is marked in red. This trail descends along the stream through the cool woodland. Visitors can see white-tailed deer on almost any visit to this sanctuary. In summer, when their antlers are growing, bucks often hang out together in small groups. The velvet-covered antlers are delicate and sensitive. In order to avoid bumping them on brush or low branches, the buck will lift his head when he runs from intruders and lay the antlers back along his neck.

Where the trail crosses the stream, look to the left for a waterfall tumbling over a series of rock outcroppings. Its beauty varies according to the amount of water. In spring clumps of hepatica bloom among the rocks alongside the waterfall; in summer there is a clump of pointed-leaved tick trefoil. Trefoil refers to the three-part pattern of this plant's leaves; tick refers to the sandpaper-covered seed that sticks to anything that brushes against it.

Turn right at the end of the Falls Loop Trail. Bear left onto the Hidden Lake Loop Trail, paralleling a stone wall. Stay on the wider trail. An orange trail turning to the right leads to the adjacent Mildred E. Grierson Memorial Wildlife Sanctuary. If you wish to explore it, use a one-way trail in and back out, but be aware that there is said to be quicksand near the Grierson lake and stay on the trail. If you do not choose this option, the wide trail you are on will lead you back to your car.

The entrance to the Mt. Holly Nature Preserve, Indian Brook's third preserve, is located approximately 1.5 miles from the Marian Yarrow entrance on Mt. Holly Road East. This preserve's diversified habitat includes meadows with a short bluebird trail, dense forest, ledges, and swamps.

Ward Pound Ridge Reservation

Location: Cross River, New York
Distance: 2 miles
Owner: County of Westchester

Ward Pound Ridge Reservation contains every terrestrial and aquatic habitat of the region—excepting salt water. In this huge park (almost 5,000 acres) you can explore crest woods, slope forests, lowland swamps, colorful marshes, vernal pools, evergreen plantations, hemlock ravines, meadows, streams, and ponds, among others. You can relax at one of the recreational picnic areas, or explore ancient Indian petroglyphs and rock shelters deep in the hills.

Access

From I-684, take the Cross River/Katonah exit. Go east on NY 35 for 4 miles to NY 121. Turn right and drive 0.1 mile to the reservation entrance road on the left. Parking fee.

Trail

Enter the park and drive up Michigan Road, which is the first right after the toll booth. Leave your car in the parking area at the end of the road, and, from the circle, walk straight ahead on the dirt path. This is the Boone Trail. The numbered posts correspond to a self-guided nature trail leaflet, available at the Trailside Nature Museum.

Bear right at a fork. Swampy land on either side of this path sports many varieties of moss. Mosses, like ferns and fungi, reproduce by means of spores. Their spore-bearing stalks vary in color from bright green to red or brown. Each capsule has a cover to protect its spores until the weather is just right for dispersal. The capsule usually has a hinged cover, with tiny teeth around the edge. Flowering moss feels like an old-fashioned butch haircut.

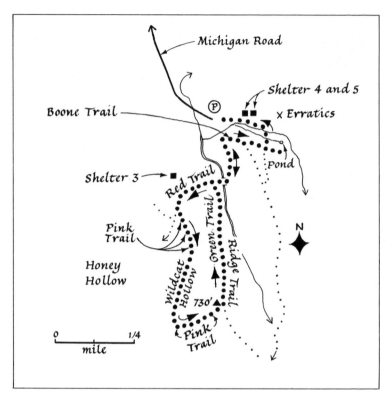

Where a stream runs under the path, skunk cabbage and marsh marigolds are abundant. Skunk cabbage is the area's earliest wildflower and can actually melt its way up through the last ice and snow. The color of the protective hood around the spathe of flowers is reminiscent of decayed meat and encourages pollination by attracting flies and beetles that normally go to such a source of food rather than to flowers. In late summer you may find skunk cabbage fruit that looks like wrinkled brown oranges lying in the mud. Each fruit contains many beanlike seeds, relished by mice and chipmunks.

Bear right at the next Y intersection onto the Red Trail. Several hundred feet along, take the Pink Trail to the left, which starts just before you see a big rock shoulder coming up on the Red Trail. The Pink Trail goes through a thick stand of laurel. Flower buds of laurel are small and flat. During winter walks you can judge where flowering will be best in

May. This thick stand makes a good hiding place for animals. It would be difficult to penetrate it, but the deer manage to get in.

You will soon approach Wildcat Hollow, a deep ravine bordered by rocks and known for the dark lushness of its hemlocks. With the demise of the hemlocks—the result of the woolly adelgid insect—what will Wildcat Hollow look like in the future? Is it possible there are really bobcats here? These animals are secretive, and none have been seen recently.

The Pink Trail becomes obscure in places and is often blocked by fallen logs. Simply follow the pink paint markers. At the beginning of a downhill portion, there is a flat area where you can walk, to the right, to an overlook above the swamp that fills this end of Wildcat Hollow. In spring you can look down on frogs chorusing their love songs in the cool sunlight. Last year's hemlock cones are crunchy underfoot. Piles of deer scat indicate that deer, as well as people, like an overlook.

Return to the trail, which continues on the left-hand side of the stream. You can leave the trail and meander back and forth according to the depth of the water. Two easily identified mosses are abundant along the way: pincushion, which is pale green-white, and fern moss, which is yellow-green and looks like a miniature fern. Pincushion is very thick and fairly dry, and it is much favored by small animals for nesting material.

Along the ravine floor, you will walk through a large stand of maidenhair fern, very evident with its fan shape and wiry black stems. Maidenhair fern is this area's only large fern with black stems, and it is fairly rare. Its habitat requirements are precise: rich, loamy soil and lots of moisture.

Because of Wildcat Hollow's constant moisture, it is a good place to look for woodland salamanders under rotten logs. Two of the area's salamanders are unusual because they do not have to lay their eggs in water. The red-backed and slimy salamanders place their eggs under logs or rocks, and the developing creatures complete the tadpole stage within their eggs, emerging as tiny salamanders. These animals are very fragile—if you pick them up by their tails, the tails may come off. If you can't resist handling them, do so carefully and return them quickly to their moist homes.

Where you can obviously go no farther in the ravine because of deadfalls, bear to the left up a hill. Look at the standing dead trees for wide furrows left by boring beetle larvae. Like termites, beetle larvae are able to consume and digest hard wood because of protozoa in their intestines that make it possible for them to gain nutrients from the wood. They are vital links in the forest's recycling chain.

At the intersection with a larger trail, turn left onto the Green Trail. After a long descent through mixed hardwood forest, you will come to the Red Trail again. Turn right, and walk back to where Michigan Road is visible. Turn right onto the other fork (the one not taken before) for a short distance, and go across a grassy path to the left. The marsh that stretches between this path and the shelter on the hillside is covered with highbush blueberry. Their red twigs, white flowers, and blue fruit make them decorative at all times of year, and they are a delicious food source for humans and other animals. Red and sugar maple, along with other tree saplings, have rooted in this blueberry and alder marsh. The walker will eventually be unable to see across the marsh to the lean-to as the swamp succeeds to deciduous forest. The lean-to shelter, by the way, is built on what some people think is a drumlin and others think is a recessional moraine. (A drumlin is a smooth, streamlined hill composed of till, deposited beneath a glacier and pointing in the direction that the glacier traveled. A recessional moraine is a mound of till that marks the margin of a glacier.) Either is a relic of sand and cobbles dumped 12,000 years ago by the last glacier. The big boulders on top, to the right of the shelter, are glacial erratics, likewise dumped.

The path leads to the edge of a hidden pond. This pond was dug for a swimming hole in the 1930s by the Civilian Conservation Corps (CCC), whose camp—practically a village—was just to the right (you can still find the old foundations). The CCC built the original museum and the camping shelters in this park. Surrounded now by shrubs, the pond is a little haven for wildlife, from fish to dragonflies and wood ducks.

Return the way you came, and watch on your right for a trail through the marsh where the fork comes down the hill on your left. This is a good birding spot, with lots of warblers in spring, redwing blackbirds, and even owls who patrol the perimeter for prey. You get a close-up look at the highbush blueberry, with their fine, twisted limbs, along with bayberry, maleberry, goldenrod, and meadowsweet. The trail will take you to the foot of the drumlin/recessional moraine. If you turn left and go to the very end of the drumlin, you will see where park staff have excavated a portion. The "hill" is just a big pile of sand. Bank swallows dig burrows near the top to nest.

On the way back to your car, remember to look for the bluebirds. To visit the park museum, drive back down Michigan Road and turn to the right. A combination of old and new, the museum not only houses materials on the wildlife and early times of the area but also has a fine library of Delaware Indian information and a wigwam encampment. You can pick up a calendar of county park events and a topographic map of Ward Pound Ridge Reservation, which has many other trails to explore. Several nice ones include a walk along the river from The Meadow Parking Area to Kimberley Bridge, a hike up the Fire Tower Trail, or a longer walk to the Leatherman's Cave.

Halle Ravine

Location: Pound Ridge, New York
Distance: 1.3 miles
Owner: The Nature Conservancy

This walk, which parallels a stream and takes you over a series of bridges, lies mostly in the depths of a ravine. Tall trees rise overhead, and visitors sometimes speak of the place's "intimate" quality—an unusual word to use about a natural area.

Halle Ravine is a jewel, filled with dark hemlocks typical of southern New York, where hemlocks are the dominant tree of such cool, moist slope conditions. At the time this revision was written, Halle Ravine's hemlocks appeared healthy. Hemlocks are dying throughout Westchester County from an infestation of the woolly adelgid, an insect introduced from Japan.

Access

From the center of Pound Ridge, go north on NY 137, and then bear north on NY 124. The first right after Hiram Halle Library is Trinity Pass Road. Go down this road 0.7 mile, and park on the edge of the road next to a white gate in a stone wall.

Trail

Go over the stone steps next to the gate, and take your first left-hand path. You will descend on a trail bordered with barberry bushes and cork-bark euonymus, landscaping plants that have been widely distributed in these woodlands by birds. When a bird eats a berry, it digests the soft material and passes the seed through its digestive system, effectively planting it along with its excrement.

Two lovely small ponds provide reflections of trees and the sound of frogs conversing with one another. In the fall, leaves sail like tiny galleons along the water's surface. One of the ravine's many decaying logs can be found near the first bridge. The damp breeze that rises from its deep cleft smells like decaying leaves and mushrooms. Many wild mushrooms are evident; slugs, squirrels, and chipmunks can eat them without harm, while one bite may prove fatal to a human.

Notice the height of these trees, which must reach extra far to get their share of sunlight. Most of the trees in this early part of the ravine are hemlock, beech, and black birch. Continue straight past the spillway and along the brook to a wooden bridge. Climb the stairs of the opposite bank and turn right to follow the trail downstream. After a short distance, a stone bench invites you to sit and look down the length of the ravine. This is only one of several pleasant meditation spots in this sanctuary.

Large flocks of crows are often found in the ravine, feeding and

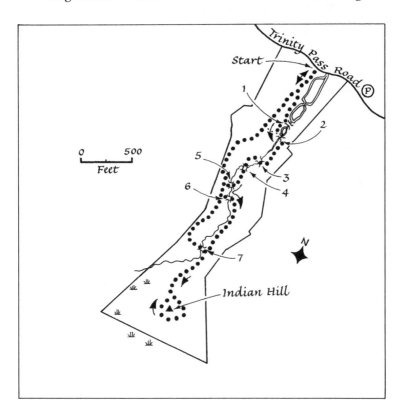

bathing in the stream. Crows have a much more organized social structure than most birds. A feeding flock usually has a lookout posted to warn them about humans or other potential danger. Long maligned as the farmer's foe, crows have been vindicated to a large degree by research that proved the birds eat a great deal of animal matter such as grubs, other insects, and mice. Crows are now protected under federal laws, although states may set hunting seasons for them. The crow is a valuable scavenger in suburban areas, feeding on the many animals destroyed by cars. However, because crows make incredible noises—caws, grindings, garglings, and strangling sounds—large winter roosts are never popular with local residents.

Near the second stream crossing are some nettles. (This is actually bridge number three on your map; you do not cross bridge number one.) You can see the nettles' stinging hairs with the naked eye, but your hand lens, carefully used, will show you the mechanism by which they work. Each hair is attached to its stem by a small bulb, and when you brush against the stem, the bulb and hair operate like a tiny hypodermic needle. The stinging can last for some time.

Remain on the path that follows the stream's edge. Beyond the fifth bridge, fine new stonework protects the edge of the stream against erosion, proving that the talent for laying dry stone walls did not die with the builders of the reservoirs.

The hemlocks end as the ravine opens and the microclimate warms. As you approach bridge six, this difference in climate is especially apparent in the dominant woodland species as they correspond to soil moisture and temperature. One bank is dark with hemlocks that extend up the hill. On the other, more level bank you'll find a stand of tulip, sugar maple, and ash trees.

Do not cross the seventh bridge yet, but continue to the end of the ravine and up over a short stone ledge into a field. You will be standing on property belonging to the town of Pound Ridge. Bear right along the field's edge. This field has some exceptional wildflowers in it, most especially fringed gentians in September and October. The beautiful fringed gentian is a biennial. It is a rosette of leaves the first year; it flowers and sets seed the second year, then dies. There are very few places left in which fringed gentian can grow, because it favors wet meadows and most of these have been developed.

In this field you will also find scouring rush, which looks like miniature bamboo or gigantic porcupine quills. The tissues of these strange, prehistoric-looking plants with green stems and no leaves contain a great deal of silica. You can feel it if you rub them with your fingers. They were named scouring rush because colonial housewives used them to clean pots and pans. The feathery field horsetail is related to this plant.

Climb a very steep hill on the other side of the field. This area is known as Indian Hill and was the site of a Native American village, one of several in the town. You may see another rare flower, yellow lady's slipper, in bloom on the hillside in May. As the path crosses the top of the hill, look for shells of white-lipped snails. This large (it has a one-inch shell) land snail is a delicacy for birds and mammals. I have found a number of shells with their central whorls chipped away and their tenants eaten. Like all snails and slugs, the white-lipped is a hermaphrodite. Each snail has both male and female sexual parts, but it must exchange genes with a partner to lay fertile eggs. The shell forms within the egg, and a newly hatched white-lipped snail is about the size of a pinhead. These snails feed on decaying vegetation.

The path goes over the top of the hill, then curves right and around the crown of Indian Hill. Watch under the hemlocks for the creeping ground cover called partridgeberry. Its twin white flowers, which appear in late June, are followed by a single red berry with two "eyes."

Return to the field and back into the ravine. Turn left and cross the seventh bridge, then turn right to bear north along the stream. The trail back is sometimes different from the one you came on and sometimes it is the same. Even when it is the same trail, it looks different because you are approaching from the opposite direction. Before you come to the stone wall by the stream and rejoin the trail to enter the ravine, look on your left for a large patch of blue cohosh, a fairly uncommon wildflower with blue-green leaves and small, star-shaped flowers. The plant bears bright blue berries in fall. These berries are highly poisonous, and not even birds eat them.

As you once again reach the stonework near the fifth bridge, turn left and, within 100 feet, watch on your left for some steps leading uphill. At the top of the second set of steps, turn right onto the Upper

Path. You will be high above the ravine, close to the tops of some of the tall trees you passed earlier. Two more inviting benches are set along this trail; you can sit and watch the activities of birds and other animals below. This ridge trail leads back to the road and your car.

Cranberry
Lake Park

Location: Harrison, New York
Distance: 1.25 miles
Owner: County of Westchester

The building of the Kensico Dam (1912–1916) had a tremendous impact on the Cranberry Lake area. The entire village of Kensico was destroyed when Kensico Reservoir was filled, and an influx of foreign workers and their families turned the little country village of Valhalla into a bustling center. Besides its natural wonders, Cranberry Lake Park is interesting for its relics from that time.

Access

Exit NY 22 at Orchard Street, 0.8 mile north of the Kensico Dam or 2 miles south of the intersection of NY 22 and NY 120. The entrance sign is on Orchard Street, 100 feet from NY 22. Parking is available.

Trail

From the parking area near the nature center, take the yellow-marked service road through the woods toward the lake. The many oak trees of the park drop acorns on the ground, and, in good years, walking the Cranberry Lake trails is like walking on marbles. White oaks bear acorns every year; red and black oaks take two years to mature their fruit. This acorn crop is very important to much of the area's wildlife. Squirrels and chipmunks depend on it for winter food supplies; deer fatten themselves on acorns for the winter. Acorns are eaten by wood ducks and blue jays, too. In years of sparse acorn production, blue jays migrate south in large numbers. When the gypsy moth population peaks every 10 years or so, the oaks expend so much energy putting out two sets of leaves that they cannot set fruit.

Continue past the first white-marked trail to the second trail, which is marked in orange. Turn left down the hill to the edge of Cranberry Lake. A short jaunt on a boardwalk takes you out to the water. Look for ospreys fishing in spring and fall. These large hawks often migrate over inland lakes. After it dives into the water to capture a fish in its strong talons, the osprey will not immediately kill its prey. Instead, the bird flies while holding the fish in a torpedolike position until it is dead.

Turn right onto the powder blue–marked trail (if faded, the paint marker appears gray), and follow along the lakeshore. You will pass gigantic growths of royal fern and bushes of speckled alder, highbush blueberry, mountain laurel, and swamp azalea. Few flowers smell more exotic than the swamp azalea. An interesting plant called downy false foxglove can be seen here in early summer. Notable for its beautiful yellow flowers, the plant is actually a parasite on the roots of oak trees. The spikes of brilliant blue flowers blooming in shallow water are pickerel weed. Pickerel may like to hide among the pickerel weed's underwater stems.

The blue-marked trail bears right up a short, steep hill. Turn left at the top, and remain on the blue-marked trail. You can see the lake when the leaves have fallen from the trees.

A fascinating insect called a pellucid wasp can often be seen in these woods, flying low among the shrubs. These wasps feed on wood-boring beetle larvae. They have very long (two to three inches) ovipositors trailing behind them. Ovipositors are egg-laying appendages that look like gigantic stingers but are actually used for drilling into dead wood and finding beetle larvae. After an egg is laid, it will hatch into a wasp larva and will feed on the larvae of the beetle.

Yellow Lady's Slipper

Just before Post 5, the trail passes through a veritable corridor of sweet pepperbush shrubs. The strong fragrance of this blooming, shoreline shrub is said to have told

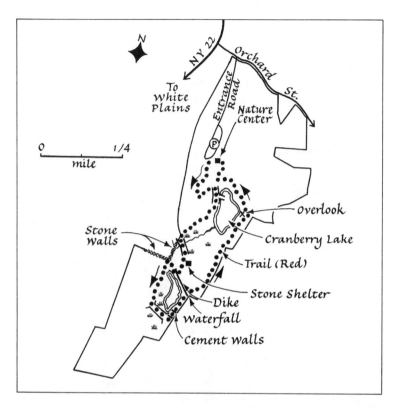

early sailors that they were nearing land. Turn left onto the dirt road, and observe the dry-laid and perfectly aligned stone wall along the right-hand side. Many of Westchester's beautiful stone walls were built by skillful masons brought to this country from Italy, Ireland, and Scotland to build the area's great dams—the Croton and the Kensico.

Turn left onto the orange-marked trail past clumps of pink lady's slipper orchids that bloom in May. Within a few yards you will come to a boardwalk, where you can clearly see that the lake is turning into a marsh. Hummocks with sedges, ferns, blueberry bushes, and red (or swamp) maple saplings are abundant. The rare calopogon orchid glows pink on the hummocks in July. White water lily blooms in the water. Floating on the water's surface is a tiny but interesting plant called bladderwort, which has yellow flowers in July. Bladderwort uses the bladders on its underwater stems to siphon in small animals, which the

Few natural cataracts, such as this one at Cranberry Lake Park,
exist in Westchester.

plant then digests. This is a good place to look for bird activity over the
lake and for sunning water snakes near the stream (the snakes are
harmless—water moccasins are not found in New York). The path from
the end of the boardwalk will lead you to a park mystery. The stone
structure along the trail may have been built for a farmhouse root cellar
(it seems evident that a house was here because of the abundance of day
lilies), a hideaway for slaves during the underground railway period, or
a storage place for the Kensico dam workers.

This path leads to a dike that separates the park's two ponds. The dike was part of a transportation system for granite quarried from North Quarry on the eastern border of the park and carried by train to the dam construction site on the other side of NY 22. The old pilings in this upper pond were part of a trestle for the train. The Kensico Dam is unusual in that it was finished several years ahead of schedule. It's worth visiting after your walk and is just a short distance south on NY 22. An area called the Dam Plaza is also a county park. Mixed waters from all members of the great Catskill and Adirondack aqueduct systems are in Kensico Lake.

At the upper pond, which is shallower than Cranberry Lake, spotted and painted turtles can usually be seen sunning themselves on logs. Painted turtles are so-called because their heads have yellow stripes and their shells have red and yellow stripes along the edges. They are one of the area's most common turtles, and they favor shallow ponds. As they lie in the sun, these turtles digest their food of water plants and small water animals. The heat of the sun is necessary for digestion because they have no internal heat of their own.

Turn right onto the dike, then left onto the powder blue–marked path that leads along the edge of the upper pond. Just past a crossing in a stone wall grows a large patch of princess pine on your left. This lycopodium or club moss looks like miniature pine trees, some of which sprout candelabras on top that bear spores for reproduction, as in ferns and mosses. The spores are ripe by fall. Shake one and see the yellow clouds come out. These spores are highly explosive. Before the days of electric bulbs they were used to make flash powder for cameras. Club mosses are on New York State's list of protected plants; they reproduce very slowly and are almost impossible to transplant. They grow abundantly where they find conditions to their liking, but those conditions are very difficult to reproduce in artificial situations.

The trail leads to another boardwalk. As you step off the boardwalk, look to your right for pink lady's slipper. If you want to see more of these famously gorgeous wild orchids, ask the park naturalist to direct you to North Quarry, where the soil is literally littered with lady's slipper in May. Turn left at the end of the boardwalk. The cement walls on the right are the foundation remnants of rock crushers and loaders used to place quarry stone onto train cars.

At the next intersection is a lovely waterfall. Turn over rocks in the stream to hunt for caddisfly larvae, whose homemade pebble houses are saliva-glued to the rock undersides. Turn over rocks beside the stream to find red-backed salamanders. Walk over the stream to continue, then bear right, again on the red-marked trail. Climb the hill through mountain laurel to an overlook from which you can see the lake/marsh spread before you. Continue on the red-marked trail to the bottom of the hill and then left along the powder blue– and green-marked trails. If at any point during your ramble through Cranberry Lake you feel in doubt about your location, the green-marked trail always marks the return to your car.

Bear left again along a trail that parallels the Cranberry Lake shore. This fairly wet and brushy area is excellent for birding, especially during spring migration. Follow the green markers to the parking area. Back at the nature center you will find exhibits of local flora and fauna, with a naturalist in attendance Wednesday through Sunday year-round.

Marshlands
Conservancy

Location: Rye, New York
Distance: 1.5 miles
Owner: County of Westchester

The Marshlands Conservancy may be the jewel of the county park system. The childhood home of John Jay, America's first chief justice of the Supreme Court, Marshland's great variety of habitat—woodland, field, and seashore—provides something of interest at every season. Marshlands also has a small museum with exhibits of local flora and fauna, including saltwater aquariums in which you can see some sea creatures up close. Educational public programs are held every weekend of the year. After a 13-year, grassroots battle against encroaching development that threatened the existence of the sanctuary, an adjacent 23 acres were acquired to ensure the continuing preservation of Marshlands. Pre–Civil War buildings were also acquired and will be rehabilitated to house a new visitors center and museum.

Access

From I-684, take NY 287 east to Exit 11, Rye. Go right (south) on US 1 for 2.6 miles. The conservancy entrance sign is on the left, just past the Rye Golf Club. Parking.

Trail

Beginning behind the museum, the trail goes first through a grove of crab apple trees. The colors of their blossoms and, later, of their fruit are various and beautiful. These trees provide fruit long into the winter for birds and mammals. As you enter the woodlands, you will be surrounded by sweet gum trees. The sweet gum, with its star-shaped leaves and spiky fruit, is more common in wet areas farther to the south; but here you'll find an almost-pure stand of this handsome tree.

Smashing waves and grinding ice have helped shape the dramatic rocks of the Long Island Sound shore.

This land was once a private estate (the John Jay homestead), and it supports many exotic plants. A huge tree trunk, on the ground to the left of the trail, was once a sweet or mazzard cherry, one of the biggest ever seen. Look at its standing stump, and you can see that the tree has been riddled by carpenter ants, which chew galleries in the wood. Carpenter ants do not actually ingest the wood—they feed on other insects and use the tree as a home—so there are piles of sawdust on the ground under the fallen trunk, an indication of ongoing ant tunneling. When wood is infested with termites there is no sawdust. Termites are able to digest wood because of bacteria that live in their intestines.

Ignore the side trail on the left. Bear left at the next fork, then right at the fork after that. Cross a raised plank walk over a wet area to emerge at the edge of a large field. At one time this was a wheat field; then it became a small airfield. Since World War II it has been allowed to grow naturally, except for annual mowing and occasional regulated burns. Natural selection under these conditions has resulted in a spectacular and interesting prairielike field of orange butterfly weed, goldenrod, sunflowers, and purple asters. The tall and rough-leaved sunflowers, grown in the gardens of Native Americans for centuries, are the original precursors of larger, modern sunflowers.

Following along the edge of the field, you will find yourself walking on a small plant that looks like a grass but is actually path rush. The rush is not mowed because it does not grow very high. Walking on it actually improves the chances of its seeds reaching the ground so they can sprout. The rush, found in a place where many feet pass by, helps prevent erosion of the trail.

Bear to the left as you approach the bend at the end of the field, and walk out to an overlook above the marsh. Spread before you is a vast harvest of marsh grasses. As winter storms mat down and tear at the marsh grasses, they become the basis for a thick, delicious soup of zooplankton, which begin the food chain for millions of organisms living here. These tiny zooplankton become food for fingerling fish that spend their early lives in such protected areas. Crabs, mussels, clams, snails, and many other creatures live and feed in the marsh. If the tide is low, the exposed mud flats may be covered with fiddler crabs, small animals that live in holes in the mud. The males have one much-enlarged claw that

they wave enticingly in the faces of the females and that they also use to fight off other males.

This is one of the best places anywhere to see snowy and great egrets, great blue herons, and night herons (both black- and yellow-crowned). The birds feed on marsh animals at low tide; at high tide they roost in the trees on small islands near the marsh's edge.

Return to the trail from the overlook, bear left, and follow the path downhill between dense thickets of catbrier and wild grape. You will soon be at the level of the marsh, walking on a low dike with the marsh on your left and a bay on your right. A beautiful tall grass here (past the tall phragmites reed) is called switch grass. Marsh mallow, with velvety soft, gray-green leaves, blooms along the dike edges in June. Marshmallows were originally made from the roots of this plant. The dike goes out to Marie's Neck, which you can circle in either direction. Be very careful of the poison ivy—it grows in this sandy location like a three-foot hedge.

At the southwesternmost point of this walk is a side trail loop through marsh grasses called *Spartina* and along the water's edge on stepping-stones. You can find many plants here that are specially adapted to saltwater marshes, including sea lavender, salt marsh pickle, salt hay (the short *Spartina* grass that gets covered by water only twice a month on the lunar tides), and cordgrass (the long *Spartina* grass that gets covered by the daily tide). The stepping-stone path winds past tidal pools filled with spent oyster and mussel shells, seaweeds, and marsh fish basking in the sun.

At last you will reach the seashore itself, with beautiful rock outcroppings of mica schist glittering in the sun. Along the beach or caught up in the grasses you may see cast-off shells of horseshoe crabs, those ungainly monsters of the sea that have remained unchanged in form and function for millions of years. In late May and early June, horseshoe crabs come to this beach during nighttime high tides to mate and lay their minute blue eggs. The sanctuary runs field trips to view this behavior.

The deeper waters of Milton Harbor host ducks of many kinds, along with herring and great black-backed and ring-billed gulls. A population explosion of starfish occasionally provides fun and games for these birds. Cormorants swim in the harbor, sometimes with just their heads and necks showing above the water, or they may sit on pilings drying their wings.

Tides bring a lot of human garbage. This park's naturalist never goes anywhere without a garbage bag and sees to it that this shoreline is one of the cleanest anywhere. (She will gladly give you a bag if you would like to help.)

Retrace your steps to the edge of the field. You can choose to walk back through a different woodland path or along the edge of the field itself. Pheasants may fly squawking away or an osprey may circle overhead. Great horned owls nest in the sanctuary, probably feeding on rabbits from this field. A last small bridge leading into the woodland toward the museum is guarded by a beautiful English oak. Along this bit of trail you can also see European sycamore, or plane trees, and turkey oaks, whose acorn cups are decorated with long bristles.

Fairfield
County

Collis P. Huntington
State Park

Audubon Center in Greenwich

Location: Greenwich, Connecticut
Distance: 1.5 miles
Owner: National Audubon Society

The Audubon Center, which has a wonderful shop and a great variety of habitats for visitors to enjoy, also offers an interpretive section with exhibits, an observation window by the bird feeders, and a teachers' resource area. Its summer Ecology Camp for adults is well known.

Access

From I-684, exit at NY 22, Armonk. Go north on NY 22 to a stoplight. Turn right onto NY 433. Continue 2.5 miles to the center (on the left). Parking. Admission charge.

Trail

From the parking lot, walk down the paved road, turn left, and take the trail on the left (not the Discovery Trail) that leads past the remains of an orchard. These old apple trees attract many birds. Birdhouses around the edge of the orchard are used by bluebirds, tree swallows, and house wrens. Look on the trunks of the trees for rows of little holes made by the yellow-bellied sapsucker, a woodpecker that drinks sap and eats small insects attracted to the sap.

At the next sign for the Discovery Trail and Mead Lake, turn right into the woodland, past a small vernal (springtime) pond. Pools of temporary water, such as this one, provide vital habitat to many spring-breeding amphibians and insects, including wood frogs, toads, spring peepers, spotted and Jefferson salamanders, and fairy shrimp.

Turn left at the fork, past an enormous dead tree cut and left lying beside the trail. This trail will take you down to the edge of Lake Mead.

Turn left at the bottom of the hill. Where the trail bends right, there is a huge patch of bloodroot. Its white flowers appear in early April, when the plants' leaves are folded around their stems. After the flower petals have dropped, the leaves unfold and continue to expand. The seeds of the bloodroot bear an unusual appendage common to most seeds of the poppy family. It is a white, succulent-looking protuberance called a caruncle, and its function for the seed is debated. Some people believe it absorbs moisture, increasing the seed's chance of sprouting. Others think it is attractive to ants, and that the ants, in removing the caruncle, scratch the seed coat and thus improve the seed's ability to sprout.

At the next intersection, turn right onto the boardwalk. Ferns grow in a junglelike fashion on the hummocks in the water. Poison sumac, one of the shrubs seen here, is rarely observed from dry land because it grows only in wet places. Poison sumac's compound leaves have no teeth and are not as numerous as those of the staghorn and other red-fruited sumacs. Its leaflets are egg shaped, with a long, pointed tip. Poison sumac develops white berries that hang like little bunches of grapes, very much like the berries of poison ivy. Also like poison ivy, this sumac can cause dermatitis in humans, so look but don't touch. In fall the shrub turns a marvelous shade of orange, blazing away in its watery oasis.

Dragonflies zoom in to land on the boardwalk's handrails. These beautiful insects spend several years of their lives in the water as nymphs. When they are ready to become adults, they crawl onto land, cling to a rock or plant stem, split down the back, and emerge with wings. Adults and nymphs both feed on other insects.

Look down into the pools for small frogs that retain some of their tadpole-stage tails. For most species, the amazing transformation from larva to adult takes place in July. The dramatic caterpillar-to-butterfly metamorphosis takes place in the pupa, while the insect is not visibly active. But in the tadpole-to-frog case, the entire configuration of the animal changes while it is still swimming about. The mouth changes, lungs take the place of gills, even the intestinal system changes from the long, involved system of a plant eater to the shorter one of an insect eater. Stored food in the tail is absorbed during the last stages of this change.

Some of the exposed rocks or plant roots around the boardwalk are good places for basking water snakes, which are aggressive if they are

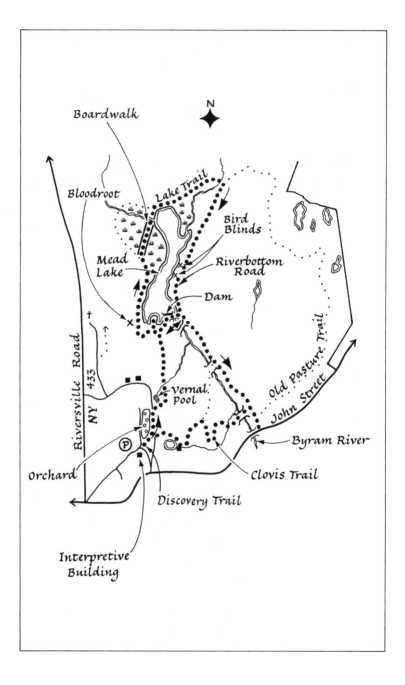

Old apple trees are some of nature's most beautiful sculptures.

picked up. Their tiny teeth can make pinholes in your skin, but no harm will come of it because the snakes are not venomous. One of their usual activities is eating those little frogs; but small water snakes are often readily eaten by bullfrogs, which will snap at anything that moves, including one of their own kind.

Other animals that may swim right under your feet include spotted and snapping turtles. Spotted turtles are becoming very scarce. The same cannot be said for snappers. I saw a huge one here, with a head the size of a human fist.

Turn right at the end of the boardwalk. Cross the stream that feeds into the lake, and continue to take each right-hand fork to follow along the lakeshore. Stop at the first bird blind. You can sit quietly here, observing the activity among hummocks and shrubs in the water. Perhaps a wood duck will swim quickly by. A phoebe builds a nest inside this blind, so leave the panels over the observation slits open.

Continue along the lake to the dam. This is a fairly high dam, and you can walk on top of it to enjoy the water thundering over and splashing up as it hits the V-shaped rock below. There are liverworts on the rocks near the edge of the dam. Examined with a hand lens, liverworts look like reptilian skin. These are ancient plants, somewhere between mosses and ferns in development, with similar reproductive cycles.

Climb off the dam, and continue down the wide trail paralleling the Byram River. Cross the river over the third bridge at the sign for the Clovis Trail. At its end, turn left on the Discovery Trail. You will come to a small pond, then to the lawns close to the cluster of buildings, and then back to the place the walk began.

Fairchild Wildflower Garden

Location: Greenwich, Connecticut
Distance: 2.3 miles
Owner: National Audubon Society

Originally developed as a special place for wildflowers, Fairchild Garden also offers a trail to a river, a spectacular gorge, wet meadows, and a pond.

Access

Exit I-684 at NY 22, Armonk. Go north to a stoplight and turn right onto NY 433. Continue 4.4 miles to North Porchuck Road (the second left after the Audubon Center in Greenwich). Follow this road 0.5 mile to the entrance on the right, identified by its green gates. Park inside the gates.

Trail

From your car, walk along Fairchild Road, left past the entrance shelter. In front of the wall through which Beech Trail passes grows galax, with round, leathery leaves. This plant usually grows farther south. On the right is a pond that can be scanned for herons and turtles.

Continue on Fairchild Road. You will soon come to a small meadow that is in the process of succeeding to woodland. Bayberry and maleberry grow there. Bayberry leaves have a wonderful smell, but they are not the bay used in cooking. The berries, waxy and gray, are used to make bayberry candles. Maleberry looks very much like blueberry, but instead of berries, its fruits are dry, brown capsules. These two field-pioneer species, which require full sunlight for growth, can be expected to be phased out as young trees take root.

Turn left, at a very large red cedar, onto Gray Glen Road. Because

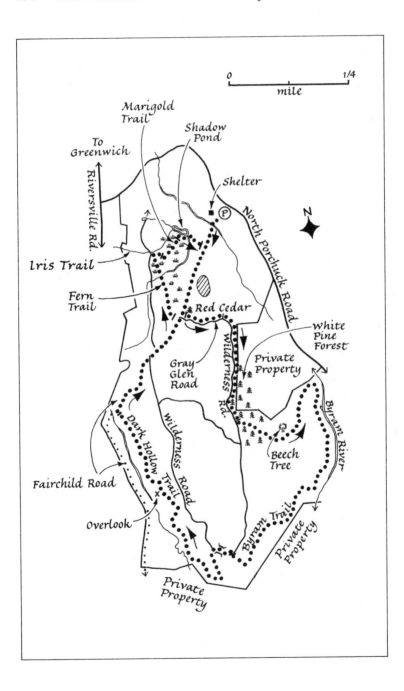

red cedar is a pioneer tree, usually growing in old fields and soon shaded out by black birch and maple, it is remarkable to see so many large red cedars in these woods. The bark, which may be shredded by squirrels, makes good nesting material; perhaps it even helps reduce the number of fleas and other vermin, just as the wood of red cedar keeps moths out of human clothes.

Listen for the crowing of a cock pheasant. These handsome birds were imported from China to England and then to North America. They seem comfortable living close to human beings. Ground-nesting birds are very susceptible to nest destruction by foxes, raccoons, and dogs—one reason unleashed dogs are unwelcome in wildlife sanctuaries.

Turn right onto Wilderness Road. This planted stand of white pines is home to little red squirrels, smaller and more aggressive than gray squirrels. Piles of pine cone scales under the trees show where they have been feeding. In addition to the chatter of squirrels, the forest offers the sound of wind high in the trees and the fragrance of needles underfoot.

Turn left onto the Byram Trail. As you descend through the pines you will enter a grove of beech trees. Scattered at their bases are beechdrop plants, parasites on the roots of beech trees. The beechdrop, which has no chlorophyll, is red and white when first in bloom, drying to brown. Apparently it does no harm to the roots on which it grows. An abundant wildflower along this trail is wild sarsaparilla, with two compound leaves on a woody trunk. In May an umbel of greenish flowers grows on a separate stalk from the leaves; it is followed by blue berries in midsummer. The roots of this plant used to be an ingredient in root beer.

The Byram River, originating in many small swamps and ponds, achieves a good width and flow here. It contains many beautiful rocks, little rapids, and pools. Very early in spring you will see stone flies on the rocks and tree trunks along the river. Stone fly nymphs live in cold rushing waters; the adults survive a very short time, just long enough to reproduce. These insects are a favorite food of trout.

Byram Trail bends away from the river. Cross a stone wall and turn right. The trail goes up and follows a long slope with many dead trees on the ground. Such fallen wood provides a good medium for a variety of mushrooms. When you reach Wilderness Road once more, turn to the

Ice forms first around rocks and along slow-running edges of the Byram River.

left. Go a short distance and take the trail on your left that turns steeply downhill. This is Dark Hollow Trail. At the bottom of the hill, the trail turns to the right. It then rises along the rim of a deep gorge sparkling with granitic mica schist, one of the basic rocks of the area. At the very top of the hill is an overlook where you can rest and watch waterfalls coming down the other side of the gorge (unless you visit during a dry season). Beside the overlook is a large witch hazel bush, another native plant formerly used for medicinal purposes and now largely replaced by chemicals. Witch hazel is the last of this area's shrubs to flower. In October it is covered with yellow flowers that have threadlike petals, and, at the same time, the fruits from the previous year are maturing. As these fruits ripen, their inner membranes shrink. Finally, with a loud pop the outer covering bursts, and hard black seeds are thrown several feet from the parent plant.

Continue on Dark Hollow Trail along the ravine edge. At the end of the Dark Hollow Trail turn right onto Fairchild Road once again.

Continue for some distance on Fairchild Road, past intersections, until you reach a left turn onto narrow Fern Trail. This trail will lead you into the wet meadow. Many blue flags and large patches of mayapple bloom here in spring. In late summer the field is ablaze with goldenrod, and the pink-and-white flowers of arrow-leaved tearthumb stick up at all angles over the goldenrod. (If you wonder why it is called tearthumb, run your fingers lightly up a stem.) Large clumps of purple ironweed and the reddening leaves of the white-fruited, gray-stemmed dogwood shrub add more color. At the end of Fern Trail is a bench where you can sit and be scolded by catbirds in the shrubbery. Turn right onto the Iris Trail, then left onto the Marigold Trail, which will bring you to the side of Shadow Pond and then back to Fairchild Road near the parking area.

Greenwich Point Park

Location: Old Greenwich, Connecticut
Distance: 1.5 miles
Owner: Town of Greenwich

Fairfield and Westchester counties' saltwater shoreline was privately developed long ago, so the public's enjoyment of diverse and exciting Long Island Sound is limited. The Town of Greenwich bought Greenwich Point from New York Presbyterian Hospital in 1945 for $550,000. While the Point is open to the general public only in winter, you must take advantage of visiting what is perhaps the finest stretch of ocean frontage in the region. Other city parks on the Sound can be silty or muddy, but Greenwich Point Park is one big stretch of natural, shining sand and cobble beach.

Access

Take Exit 5 off I-95. Turn east onto Putnam Avenue for 0.3 mile. Turn right onto Sound Beach Avenue and drive 1.8 miles through Old Greenwich. Turn right onto Shore Road. Proceed 0.6 mile to where the road narrows as it becomes Tods Drift Way. Keep straight across the causeway for 0.2 mile to the entrance booth. Continue 0.6 mile through the park to the Holly Grove. Parking.

Note: Park open to the general public only from December 1 to April 14. Resident pass required from April 15 to November 30.

Trail

Be sure to dress warmly—the sea-beach is always windy and feels cooler than the inland. Time yourself for low tide when beachcombing is at its best. As you motor through the entrance gate, you may be tempted to stop at the first sign of sand and bright ocean light. Go right ahead. You might also want to drive around the point first, taking in the sights. When

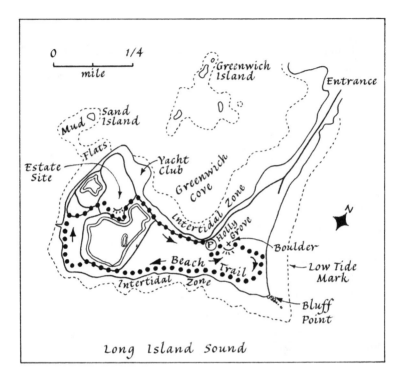

you're ready, park at the Holly Grove by the totem pole–like sculpture.

The 21 varieties of European holly found here were a gift to the park from Mr. and Mrs. Allan Kitchel on the occasion of their fiftieth wedding anniversary in 1959. Walk beneath the entrance sign and wander through this enchanting grove of dark green foliage and red berries. Holly figures highly in the folklore of Europe. Its name means holy in old English. In ancient Italy, peasants used holly to celebrate the midwinter solstice Saturnalia. Holly was one of the seven noble sacred trees of the grove in ancient Irish law. There is a holly native to the United States, but you won't see it at Greenwich Point. Visit Woodcock Nature Center in Ridgefield and Wilton (Walk 28) to see the deciduous American holly of wet soils.

Search the ground beneath the trees for owl pellets. Owls swallow their prey whole or in large pieces. The owl's stomach digests the meat, but the bones, nails, teeth, beaks, feathers, or fur are compressed into a ball that the owl then regurgitates. If you find one of these gray pellets and pull it apart, you can tell exactly what the owl ate—you may even be able to reconstruct a vole, mouse, or bird skeleton.

Saw-whet owls winter within the protective cover of this grove. At eight inches high they are North America's smallest owl, so their regurgitated pellets are tiny. You can try peering through the prickly foliage, but you most likely will not see an owl. Rest assured, however, that the owl will see you. Although they are strictly nocturnal, owls do not sleep one wink from birth to death. Daytime is simply spent resting motionless yet alert.

At the end of the grove, bear left on all trails you meet. White-throated sparrows—winter residents that have flown south from Canada and the mountains of New England—sing "Old Sam Peabody, Peabody, Peabody" within the tangled underbrush of honeysuckle and bittersweet. Walk past black cherry, sugar maple, and Norway maple trees. The trail bends left as if you are going back to your car. At the T intersection with a wide trail, turn right to visit the Memorial Boulder.

This big rock originally lay beside Greenwich Cove. It was hauled to this site to commemorate the life of J. Kennedy Tod, who lived on the point. Plaques describe the founding of the Town of Greenwich in 1640 and the sale of land from coastal Siwanoy Indians for the price of 25 English coats, a shrewd bargain even in those days. During the early phases of European–Native American contact, neither side understood the land beliefs of the other. To the Natives, land "sales" were merely leases for land use—sometimes quite specific uses, for example, for wampum-making only or for beach-plum picking only. The grantors always maintained the right to visit and likewise use the land as needed. Monakewaygo is the Paugussett name for Greenwich Point, which a recent linguist translates to mean "deep at the end" or "deep at the point's end" or "plenty of meat." Others have said the word means "shining sands."

Before you spreads a view of the sun-glittering sound. Face away from the boulder and head left across the picnic area toward a service road. Cut across the road to the beach, and turn right for Bluff Point. You can either use the Beach Trail or, depending on the tide, walk the beach itself. If you walk on the beach, be careful not to trample any plants.

The air smells of salt and sea wrack. It may be cold in winter, but marine animals and plants are still there for us to find. At first glance, a beach is simply a strip between ocean and land. However, this ecotone (edge between ecosystems) is complex and composed of distinct habitats populated by highly adapted plants and animals.

The intertidal zone is the shore area between the highest spring tides and the lowest spring tides. A spring tide is a tide of maximum range that occurs at the times of the new and full moons. Within this zone, organisms are subjected to daily inundation by seawater, desiccation, heat, freezing, and dilution by rain or runoff. It's a tough place to live. This zone at Greenwich Point can be subdivided into high and low rocky intertidal zones characterized, respectively, by barnacle and sea wrack, and high and low salt marsh zones, which in turn are characterized by two *Spartina* grasses.

Barnacles begin life when they hatch in spring from eggs held inside their hermaphroditic parent. The local currents sweep them away. They feed and molt once, then by April or June are ready to settle down. They choose a hard substrate, whether shell, rock, or piling, and cement the tops of their heads to it. They then grow their limestone shell, usually made of six side plates and a pair of movable top plates that open for feeding and reproduction. They are, as Louis Agassiz described in the 1800s, "nothing more than a little shrimp-like animal, standing on its head in a limestone house and kicking food into its mouth."

When the top plates are shut, a barnacle can survive prolonged exposure to direct sun, rain, and freezing conditions. The conical shape of the shell allows waves to crash over the rocks with forces of up to 40 pounds per square inch without dislodging the animal. Despite this, no barnacle can withstand the weight of a human, so don't walk on them. In winter the barnacle is actually warmer than the surrounding air. The sunlight warms it, and the creature retains seawater within its body to keep itself from freezing. When the tide covers the rocks, the barnacle opens its top plates and uncurls its feeding filter-fans, which sweep the water for microscopic food particles.

There are many barnacles covering the rocks at Bluff Point, an indication of the availability of barnacle food and good protection from waves and temperature fluctuations. Living among the barnacles, farther down the zone toward the water, are its two main competitors, blue mussel and brown sea wrack. The closer to the water, the more the mussels. Blue mussels cannot tolerate exposure to air as well as barnacles. Mussels are usually only found living with barnacles in moist, protective crevices among the rocks. Like the barnacle, a blue mussel starts life as a free-floating larva swept away from its parents on spring currents. Between June and September the young mussel sinks to the bottom of the ocean and metamorphoses into a miniature mussel. The animal makes its way upshore with its foot and anchors itself to the hard substrate of its choice by means of threads called byssal threads. If the lines get broken by the waves, the mussel simply spins new ones. If the mussel does not care for the place it chose, it can cast off its threads and move to another spot. The mussel, a bivalve mollusk, eats by siphoning water through its mucous-coated gills, trapping food particles and passing them to its mouth. Blue mussels always look blue and polished because they regularly clean themselves with their foot.

Among this community of barnacles and mussels, oysters can be found, along with herbivorous periwinkle snails grazing like cows upon the algae. Both of these animals have fascinating life histories—I'll leave

Low tide comes in at Bluff Point.

you to explore them in your local library or bookstore.

Farther out in the lower intertidal zone, the brown sea wrack can be seen. Also known as brown algae, brown rockweed, and Fucales, the small number seen in the intertidal zone grows as the open water is reached, forming a veritable jungle that offers protection to hundreds of organisms. This seaweed is well adapted to surviving the temperature fluctuations and desiccation of exposure during low tide. It is frost-hardy, has thick cell walls to withstand water loss, and is both flexible and strong to tolerate wave action. It reproduces like an animal: The separate sexes release sperm and eggs into the water. A chemical from the egg attracts the sperm, and the fertilized egg attaches itself to a hard substrate to grow. The most common sea wrack is bladder wrack, whose bladders buoy the plant's fronds into the sunlit water for photosynthesis.

Salt marsh grows in the upper intertidal zone. Find a sandy opening and walk beside the plants (not on them). You will see how the plant stems hold mucky, solid soil in place upon the shifting sand of the beach. This muck, which absorbs water like a sponge, makes the salt marsh a valuable beach anchor and breakwater. The taller *Spartina*, known as cordgrass, grows where it is flooded by the tides twice a day. Cordgrass was used by European colonists to thatch their roofs. The shorter *Spartina*, known as salt hay, grows above the tide line, although it must be inundated at least on the spring tides if it is to survive. Salt hay was harvested as fodder for cattle, and livestock were even set to pasture in salt marshes. In summer the *Spartina* is green, but in winter it turns blond and looks like straw.

Find a sandy opening between the *Spartina* plants, and follow the beach or Beach Trail around Bluff Point. If you are walking the beach, you will find flotsam that hints at the teeming life within the deeper open water: large, round moon snail shells, slipper shells with half a bottom, jingle shells that look like shriveled human toenails, and the ubiquitous periwinkles. You'll also find crab carapaces and claws, whole or broken bits of horseshoe crabs, and whelk egg cases like long strings of coins. Across the sound stretches Long Island, and the skyscrapers of Manhattan loom into sight as you round the point.

The *Spartina* comes right up to the breakwater boulders here, so clamber up the rocks if you are on the beach and use the trail. The shrubs that line the trail are adapted to dry shore living and include bayberry and roses with red, edible rose hips. Cross a wooden bridge that lets tidewater into a salt marsh. This is actually a constructed salt marsh, planted in 1975, and the first proof in Connecticut that *Spartina* could be reestablished on a damaged site.

There is so much to look at: waves and sun, woods and golden *Spartina*, gulls patrolling the flotsam on the beach, tankers and tugs. And the birding is excellent throughout. When you can leave the trail, do so by keeping along the beachfront and walking onto the gravelly sand past mounded rows of rotting seaweed, broken *Spartina* (that looks like straw), and shells. This short section of beach soon rejoins the Beach Trail. Pass another salt marsh over two inlet bridges. The trail ends at a paved road. Turn left.

This freshwater lake is a good spot to watch diving ducks, which in winter include scaup, goldeneye, bufflehead, merganser, and horned grebe. As the road bends right around the lake, keep left along the shore past a parking area and out again onto beachfront. Walk on the sand and rocks or choose a trail that runs along the picnic area. If high tide has arrived, there may be no beach at all. This trail ends at another parking lot. Out in the bay extensive mud flats are exposed at low tide, and people with buckets dig clams. You can walk that way and try some digging yourself. The species of burrowing clam they are after is the quahog, which, at different ages and sizes, gets called various names: Youngsters are known as cherrystone; they grow into littlenecks and then into the older chowders. The inside edge of the quahog shell is purple; the remainder is white. Native Peoples laboriously shaped tiny beads from this shell, calling it wampum. The shores of Long Island were the wampum-making capital of the East Coast. Sacred meaning was (and still is) attached to the beads, which were used to seal treaties and commemorate events, used during religious ceremonies, and sewn into story belts. These belts are still used by traditional storytellers, who, perhaps once a year, bring the belts into public to "read" their stories. The purple beads— fewer in number than the white—symbolize political or social entities. The white beads usually represent the river of peace that flows past the purple characters. When Dutch colonists settled in the region, they needed a medium of exchange and turned to wampum. In Holland, *zeewan*, or Dutch wampum, was manufactured in factories in such quantities that it flooded the American market, and wampum simply turned into money.

If you are not visiting the mud flats in search of quahogs, turn right onto the paved road toward the lake, then left up the driveway that leads uphill and is lined by mortared stone walls. The remains of the estate of J. Kennedy Tod, a Scottish banker and railroad magnate who purchased Greenwich Point in 1884, can be found at the top of the hill. The point was originally two separate islands. Tod connected them with causeways and built his mansion where there is a view of the lake and the sound.

Make your way down to the paved road at the lake and turn left. At the T intersection by the yacht club, turn right to return to your car. Black ducks quietly forage in sheltered Greenwich Cove. Notice how *Spartina* salt marshes ring the land, except where humans have built structures. The roadway here is littered with fragments of clam shells from gulls who dropped their prey to break the clams open so they could reach the meat inside.

Bartlett
Arboretum

Location: Stamford, Connecticut
Distance: 0.75 mile
Owner: State of Connecticut

The Bartlett Arboretum offers a combination of natural and human-controlled environments. Its various specialty plantings—nut trees, dwarf conifers, azaleas, and rhododendrons—are of great interest to the home landscaper and amateur botanist. The greenhouse, which is cared for by volunteers, is one of the most interesting I have ever seen. Ask in the office if you would like to visit it.

Access

From the Merritt Parkway, take Exit 35 onto CT 137 north (High Ridge Road). Continue 1.5 miles, passing the Stamford Museum and Nature Center, and turn left onto Brookdale Road. Follow Brookdale to the arboretum entrance. Park at the end of the drive.

Caution: Do not take this walk if conditions underfoot are wet. Algae on the arboretum boardwalk can be dangerously slippery.

Trail

To enter the natural woodland and boardwalk area, take the Rose A. Thielens Memorial Ecology Walk (the Yellow Trail) from the parking lot. You will walk through a typical New England woodland of white oak, sugar and red maple, beech, and yellow birch. Many of the trees are labeled. Watch on your right for a large American elm tree, once a common planting along city and suburban streets. Just before the boardwalk, look on your left for three beeches growing on top of a rock. One of the trees is dead, another is half dead and rotting; both are full of interesting holes that look like good spots for raccoons or owls.

Cross the bridge over Poorhouse Brook, and look along the trail for some very large specimens of Solomon's plume, or false Solomon's seal. This plant is so-called because each year when the flowering stem dies back, a round depression that looks like a seal is left on the rhizome, its underground stem. These rhizomes are not buried very deeply, so a little scraping away of the soil will show you the "seal." True Solomon's seal, whose flowers and fruits hang from each leaf axil rather than from the end of the leaf stalk as in the false variety, grows here, too.

Turn right, walk downstream a hundred feet or so past a stone wall, and turn left to follow the yellow arrow. There are dead logs in the woods here. These logs are important to the small animal life of the forest. In summer they are daytime hiding places for millipedes, sow bugs, and centipedes, as well as red-backed salamanders. If you like to pick up such creatures for closer examination, watch out for the centipedes. These flat,

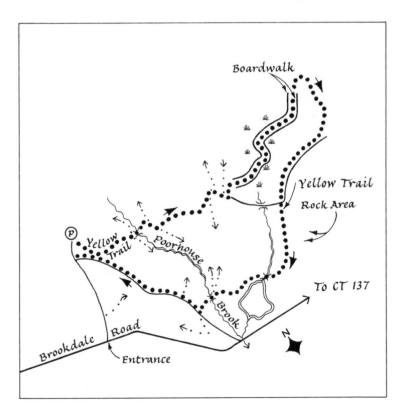

reddish animals are predators of insects and other small animals. They can bite rather hard, and they have a poison in that bite that will make your finger sting for several hours. Centipedes are very fast moving animals because they are predatory, unlike the rounded, brown millipedes that only feed on decaying plants.

In winter, logs like these are hibernating places for animals such as the white-faced hornet queen. The queen is the only member of the hornet community to survive the winter. In early spring she emerges from her hibernating log and begins to build a paper nest. As she lays eggs and raises workers, the nest slowly grows. When there are enough workers to supply the colony with food and building material, the queen stays in the nest and continues to lay eggs. She is fed by the workers, who feed on other insects. The paper nest may grow to the size of a football or even larger. When cold weather arrives, all the inhabitants of the nest, except the queen, will die. The nest is never used a second time. It is often torn apart by woodpeckers seeking larvae and pupae that may remain in the nest at the end of the season.

Follow the trail past the logs to see large masses of wood anemone blooming in April. At the intersection, turn left and then immediately right, still following the yellow arrows. At the next intersection, the yellow arrows again point you left and then immediately right. You will approach a wonderful boardwalk that runs at a height of several feet through a swamp. The red pine of the boardwalk grows algae, so if the boards feel at all slippery when you step on them, please stay off.

One of the major plants in this swamp is arrow arum, a relative of skunk cabbage and jack-in-the-pulpit. Its flowers, on a stalk called a spadix, are hidden inside a long, green spathe. As the seeds ripen, the stem holding them gracefully bends down into the mud, planting the seeds in their preferred habitat. Other beautiful swamp plants to see are speckled alder, sweet pepperbush, silky dogwood with white flowers or blue berries, large clusters of royal and sensitive fern, and winterberry, a deciduous holly with inconspicuous flowers but blazing red fruit. In late summer the cardinal flower contributes its bright red flower stalks to the scene.

Turn right at the end of the boardwalk, and follow the blue arrows. The edges of this woodland trail will be covered with white woodland aster in late summer. Evergreen plants such as spotted wintergreen and partridgeberry are here, too. Turn right at the intersection. Where the wide woodland road turns right, continue left on the Yellow Trail. You will have to negotiate your way through what looks like a glacial dump. Rocks of all sizes are everywhere, many of them with beautiful growths of mosses and lichens. Dwarf ginseng nestles among the rocks in April. Bear right at the fork. This trail crosses a bridge over the inlet to a pond.

Continue on the Yellow Trail along the edge of the pond, following the yellow arrows and triangles. When you come to the pond bank, the Yellow Trail turns sharply right, goes across an open area bounded by a stone wall, and then goes left across Poorhouse Brook. Turn right onto a service road. This hillside is an extravaganza of daffodils in spring. The road will take you back to the entrance road, from which you may explore the arboretum's many specialty gardens.

You might like to combine your visit to Bartlett with a visit to the Stamford Museum and Nature Center, where you can see captive wildlife such as white-tailed deer, owls, raccoons, and skunks. The museum usually has an art show along with other exhibits; there is also a planetarium. The parking fee at the museum is $5 for non-Stamford residents.

New Canaan Nature Center

Location: New Canaan, Connecticut
Distance: 1 mile
Owner: New Canaan Nature Center Association

There is so much going on at the New Canaan Nature Center that it is difficult to decide whether to walk first or to begin by exploring the center's exhibits and its horticultural building. The latter, which has a contemporary passive-solar design, is full of delightful plants.

Access

From the Merritt Parkway, take Exit 37. Go north on CT 124 for 2.8 miles. The center is on the left side of CT 124 (Oenoke Ridge Road), 0.5 mile north of town. Parking.

Trail

When you start to walk, take the path from the end of the parking lot. Cross the brook on a stone bridge and stop under tall, dark Norway spruce trees. You may turn right to visit the Wildflower Garden.

Follow the small side path that leads uphill, and turn left at the T intersection. At the next T intersection, fruit for birds is evident. Holly and viburnum bushes grow on the left and a large poison ivy vine clambers up a tree in front of you.

Turn right to follow the trail. An unusually large mockernut tree grows on your left. This tree, of the hickory family, has a nut that is almost as good as the shagbark's, but it has a thinner husk. Nuts such as these are eagerly sought by squirrels and chipmunks for winter stores. The animals remove the husks before burying or storing nuts because husks absorb water and cause the nuts inside to decay. Empty husks found on the ground in winter usually have small grubs eating away inside them.

Gray-green lichens decorate the bark of the mockernut tree. Lichens do no damage to the substrate on which they grow. They are a combination of an alga and a fungus, living in a symbiotic relationship. The fungus secretes an acid to help them hold on, and the green alga makes food that both consume. Because lichens are very sensitive to air pollution, their presence in such abundance indicates that the air of this region is fairly clean.

Listen to and look for chipmunks as you walk. When close by, a chipmunk's scolding sounds much like a little squirrel's. Sometimes you may hear an apparently distant sound like two sticks being struck together. This is a chipmunk's warning noise, which has a ventriloquial quality. I have seen chipmunks making this noise—they puff out their cheeks and keep their mouths closed. These little ground squirrels are not true hibernators. They retire underground during the winter and sleep for long periods of time, however, along their tunnels are storerooms full of nuts, berries, and seeds. If a chipmunk awakes during cold weather, it has a supply of food. Other rooms in the long tunnel system are used for nesting areas and bathrooms (wild animals do not soil their own nests).

Bear right—the left trail through the stone wall goes to a wildlife sanctuary under the auspices of the New Canaan Land Conservation Trust—and then slightly to the left. This sanctuary has many large trees, and to the left of this trail is a beech with some carving on it. The first

graffiti was probably carving on trees and scratching on rocks. Much as we deplore the practice now, it is sometimes interesting to read signs others have left. The earliest date I can find on this tree is 1946.

As is true of all former estate lands, New Canaan Nature Center has many exotic shrubs such as forsythia and euonymus. A very large, partially hollow, native white ash is on the left of the trail. Continue straight ahead to walk under a mulberry tree. Because mulberries are many birds' favorite food, these trees are often planted in orchards to keep birds away from other fruits, such as cherries, that ripen at the same time. The

Cup Plant

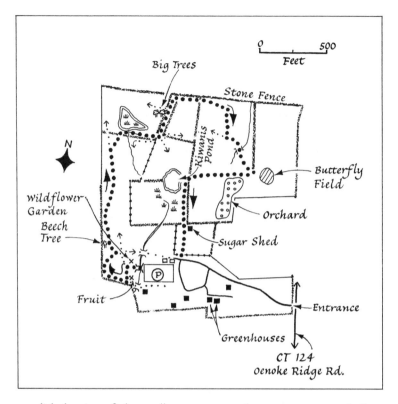

purplish berries of the mulberry tree can be very messy underfoot, however, so if you plant one to attract birds to your yard, don't put it where people walk.

Bear right toward the pond. If you approach slowly, you may see a muskrat swimming in the pond or foraging along the pond's edge. Muskrats are rodents that, like beavers, have adapted to life in the water. Their fur is soft and waterproof. Sometimes they build small lodges, beaverlike in design but made of reeds rather than sticks. More frequently they tunnel into banks or the water side of dams, a practice that does not endear them to human pond keepers. Muskrats have naked scaly tails, flattened from side to side, which they use as rudders.

Go straight ahead through the stone wall, and turn left onto an old farm road. On your left, just before the next intersection, are two gigantic trees in an open area. One is a swamp white oak, the other a red maple.

Both have girths that should make them candidates for a "Big Tree" register somewhere.

Turn right, then right again, and then left. This trail leads into an open field the nature center calls a butterfly field. Come to see the fireflies at dusk in summer. The area is mowed to keep it from reverting to forest. At one end is an orchard. Apple cider making is one of the fall events here. The trail makes a hairpin right turn, and on the right is a large stand of cup plant, one of the more unusual of the plants that resemble sunflowers. Its large leaves grow around its stem, making a cup that retains rainwater. The trail leads to the edge of the Kiwanis Pond, so-named for one of the many local organizations that contribute to the New Canaan Nature Center. The outlet from the pond makes a marshy area, with cattails and other wet-ground plants providing shelter for nesting birds.

Turn left to return to the parking area. On the way back to the main buildings you might visit the maple syrup shed, which is active in earliest spring when the sap begins to rise.

Woodcock Nature Center

Location: Ridgefield and Wilton, Connecticut
Distance: 1 mile
Owner: State of Connecticut
(leased by Woodcock Nature Center)

What's a woodcock? It is a strange-looking, swamp-living, mud-walking bird that is brown-feathered for camouflage, chunky, and has a ridiculous beak longer than an earthworm. But woodcocks are known for more than just the way they shove that beak into the mud looking for grubs. They're known for their spring dance.

On a moonlit spring night, the male woodcock spirals upward. Wind whistles through his stiff, short wings. His windsong trills louder until, in a final burst, he plummets, stately and absurd, with starlight on his wings and the moon in his eyes, to his mate on the dark, moist soil.

Woodcock Nature Center leads guided walks to spy on this creature during his mating dance. The rest of the year the center runs many educational programs for the public and the museum houses exhibits. One hundred forty-six acres of mixed deciduous woodland contain trails and a boardwalk that provide glimpses of rich wetlands replete with scarlet-berried American holly.

Access

From Ridgefield center, take CT 102/Branchville Road south and east for 1.3 miles. Turn right onto Nod Road and drive 1 mile. Turn right onto Deer Run Road. The nature center entrance is 1,000 feet down the road on the left. Drive through the white gate and park at the end of the long driveway.

Trail

From the parking lot, go behind the nature center to see the white water lilies on the human-made (see the dam?) pond. Walk left along the pond's

Winterberry, also called American holly, retains its red berries through the winter.

edge where the Red Trail begins under gray birches hanging out over the water. Just inside the tree cover, on your right, stands a large, old tree chewed by beaver and currently being recycled by multicolored fungus. You'll see more old beaver chews as you walk.

At the old field, dying red cedars are being succeeded by beech, black birch, red maple, and oaks. Tupelo and sweet pepperbush can be found along the bank. Go over a stone wall and turn left. The woods contain a lot of shagbark hickory, the nuts of which are a valuable wildlife food. People like them, too, if you can beat the squirrels to them! Some folks prefer the flavor of hickory nuts even to walnuts.

As you walk uphill, the soil becomes drier. Correspondingly, red maple disappears, black birch increases in frequency, and the woods are populated by white, black, and red oak. There is also a lot of shagbark hickory. Lowbush blueberry and huckleberry create an extensive, shrubby ground layer. The green-stemmed vine with thorns is catbrier.

Stone walls remind us that this was once pastureland. The grasslike plants found here are actually woodland sedges. Feel a sedge stem. It is triangular, while grass stems are round. The Red Trail bends left.

At the next intersection, turn right onto the Green Trail within the mountain laurel. This trail leads to bedrock outcroppings and a view through the trees of a red maple, ash, and tupelo swamp.

This is Spectacle Brook, part of the flood control area of the Norwalk River. Flooded by a dam, the swamp supports a lush shrub layer of winterberry, sweet pepperbush, dogwoods, and speckled alder. At the last ledge before the trail turns back into the woods, the ledge soil sprouts beechdrops beneath the beech trees. These pale, parasitic plants lack chlorophyll and live off the beech trees' roots.

Walk through the woods of beech, red and white oak, black birch, witch hazel, and mountain laurel. At the intersection with the Yellow Trail, bear right under the beech trees, where you'll see many parasitic beechdrops. Note how they have scales for leaves. The Yellow Trail

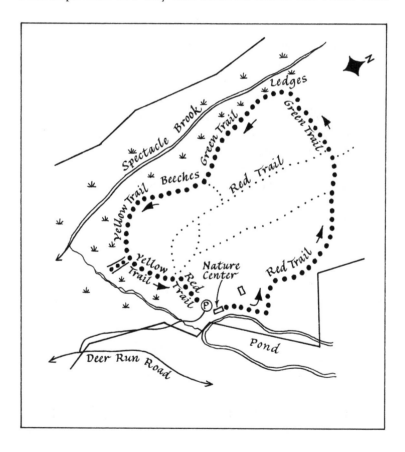

follows the edge of the swampy floodplain and takes you to the boardwalk, where you can see the swamp plants up close.

Swamps have trees. Marshes don't. Before you stretches a typical swamp of southwestern Connecticut. The dominant tree species are red maple and ash (the ash have the diamond-patterned bark and compound leaves). Spring comes first to wetlands, when the red maples bloom in April. The stocky, deep red blooms with two threadlike pistil parts are females; the red and yellow blooms are males, and their fuzzy parts are the pollen-bearing anthers. Red maple trees are usually either male or female, but occasionally they're both, half the tree male, half female. The male pollen fertilizes the female eggs, and from her two pistils grow the twin wings of polynoses, or samaras, a seed inside each.

One of the dominant shrubs in the swamp is winterberry, also called American holly and black alder. Winterberry (*Ilex verticillata*) blooms in May and has small green-white flowers that are seldom noticed. But by autumn, the bright red berries ripen and, for a while, make a fine display against the green foliage. The leaves then turn yellow and fall and, when snow blankets the land, the red holly berries are easily enough to brighten even the dreariest winter day. They last on the branches far into the cold season, sometimes even until spring, when the new leaves push them off. Robins and bluebirds eat the berries, but a flock of cedar waxwings can strip a bush in minutes, leaving the bare black branches for the remainder of the winter.

Fall at the swamp is spectacular: red and orange maple leaves, yellow and purple ash; the swamp blueberry turns scarlet and the pepperbush flames orange.

What seem to be tall grasses growing from the water and hummocks are actually sedges. Royal fern shares the hummocks. The green stuff floating on the water surface is duckweed, an important food source for waterfowl. If you pick some up, you'll see they are little, round plants with root hairs hanging from their undersides. Make certain you put them back in the water.

Sitting at the end of the boardwalk is peaceful and relaxing. The black water reflects stems, leaves, and the sky. This is also a good birding spot.

Back on land, continue along the Yellow Trail. Turn right onto the Red Trail, passing many old beaver chews, for the return to your car.

Weir
Preserve

Location: Wilton, Connecticut
Distance: 1.5 miles
Owner: The Nature Conservancy

W hen you visit Weir Preserve, you also get to stroll the grounds of Weir Farm, the first national park devoted to an American artist. Both properties are named for J. Alden Weir, the American Impressionist artist. The properties share practically the same human-use history. In fact, the sublime country-farm landscape preserved at Weir Farm is what Weir Preserve looked like before the trees grew back, transforming, through natural vegetation succession, many pastures back into woodland. All the signs of farming are still there: stone walls, farmers' rock piles, and a relatively young woodland typical of the region.

Access

From the Merritt Parkway, take Exit 39 onto US 7 north. Go 4 miles to Wilton center, turning north onto CT 33. Proceed 2 miles. Turn right onto Nod Hill Road and go 3.3 miles. The entrance is on the left; park in the pull-off.

From I-84 in Danbury, drive south on US 7 for 7 miles to a right turn onto CT 102/Branchville Road. Go 0.3 mile. Turn left onto Old Branchville Road. Go 0.5 mile to a left turn onto Nod Hill Road. Proceed 1 mile on Nod Hill Road to the preserve entrance on the right. Park in the pull-off.

Trail

Before starting down the Yellow Trail, take a look at the pond with the dead trees, across the road from the parking pull-off. This is an excellent place for birding, especially for watching ducks during migration.

Begin your walk on the old road trail. You can tell this is an old road because it is bordered by stone walls. Farmers reaped two harvests every year, it was said: crops and stones. The glacial till that was the parent material for this area's soil made for subsistence farming, and frost action brought up cobbles each spring. After clearing the land of trees, farmers spent every year clearing the soil of rocks. Sometimes they tossed the rocks into piles, but most often they used them to build walls. These dry wall fences served to keep roving swine and cattle out of crops, protected flocks within fields, functioned as boundary markers, and, to some extent, sheltered standing grain from snow drifts and summer winds. Furthermore, the condition of these walls commented on the farmer himself, as was written in 1775:

> *There is nothing can give a man, that only travels through a country, so bad an opinion of the husbandry of it, as to see two circumstances: first the fences in bad order; and secondly, the corn full of weeds.*

Building a stone wall that lasts takes skill and, some would say, is an art. Weir Preserve's walls are in good shape, despite the lack of repair since the 1800s, when fence viewers were appointed by municipalities to inspect stone walls and enforce the strict fence laws. Of course, there is no longer an agricultural reason to maintain the walls, and Nature Conservancy policy is to let nature maintain itself. A stone-lined lane such as this is typical of the small New England farm. The lane usually runs from the barnyard to the pastureland, where livestock could be turned into one of several stone-wall-bordered fields for grazing. You'll be walking through several of these old pasturelands that have since reverted to woods.

The Yellow Trail crosses a brook. At the intersection with the White Trail, you can pick up a copy of the trail map and sanctuary leaflet. Continue along the Yellow Trail through a woodland of black, red, and scarlet oak, black birch, shagbark hickory, and red maple. In about 100 yards, after crossing an intermittent stream, you will see a fallen hickory tree on your right. Notice how it pulled away from the bedrock. Look at its roots. There's no taproot! The commonly held notion that a tree has a root like a carrot that delves as deeply into the soil as the tree's trunk reaches into the sky is a myth. Tree roots are relatively shallow and

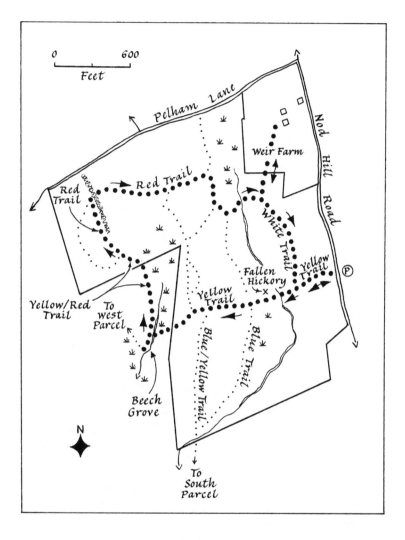

radiate horizontally from the trunk through the upper soil layers.

The trail narrows through a thick stand of twisty-trunked mountain laurel. This shrub dominates parts of the preserve in June with its magnificent blooms. Follow the Yellow Trail past intersections until you meet the Blue Trail for the second time. Vandals could not resist carving their names on the trunks of the two smooth-skinned beech trees you see here. Such is the sad fate of beech trees wherever people frequent. Two beeches that stand off the trail escaped unscathed.

The Yellow Trail forks. Turn right. As you approach the brook, soil moisture increases, and you now see yellow birch and swamp azalea. Cross the brook on stones and logs. For a small side trip, keep left to visit a small but enchanting beech grove where the parent tree is surrounded by its progeny. Return to the brook, but do not cross it. On your left, yet another fork of the Yellow Trail continues into the mountain laurel and through private property. As long as you stay on the trail, you will be fine. This trail is actually the Yellow-Red Trail.

To your right, the wetland corridor is overgrown by green-stemmed catbriers. The catbrier's hooked thorns, sharper than the claws of cats, are the most vicious the hiker can encounter. They are strong and tear not only clothing but flesh, too. The male and female vines are separate, one bearing pollen, the other bearing eggs in green flowers that ripen into blue-black berries beloved by birds. Explore the many types of mosses growing on the sedge hummocks. In late spring and early summer the sweet pepperbush and swamp azalea bloom, perfuming the air.

You will pass a jut of bedrock on the left. A black birch grows on

The stone walls at Weir Farm were built with rocks the farmers cleared from the soil every year.

top and sends a remarkably long root the entire length of the bedrock. A bit farther, a large granitic-gneiss boulder sits in the trail. Since it was only recently exposed to the elements, its surface has hardly weathered. Unlike the homogenous gray-green cortex of the rocks in the stone walls, this boulder displays all its minerals: shiny mica, white crystalline quartz, and feldspar.

Where the Red Trail forks, keep straight. Follow a stone wall, then go through it into a woodland that, compared to the other areas you've passed, only recently grew from an abandoned field. The young trees, the presence of highbush blueberry and red cedar (which only grow in full sunlight), and the long, horizontal limb on the sugar maple at the wall crossing are clues that this woodland was once a field. Within this enclosure are many witch hazel trees. Normally, witch hazel is called a shrub, but here it's a small tree. These trees bloom in fall, when most other plants produce seeds. Once you've smelled the autumn-subtle yellow, spiderlike blooms of witch hazel, you can identify its proximity simply by the honey-sweet odor in the air on a sunny day. Oil distilled from the inner bark makes a popular sore-muscle remedy. A rod of witch hazel with a crotch was the original divining rod.

The trail snakes an S curve through rocks and stone walls. More good stonework can be seen where seepage has been formed into a spring. The Red Trail ascends slightly uphill, and the soil moisture lowers. Correspondingly, oaks, black birch, sugar maple, mountain laurel, and lowbush blueberry predominate. There also are several dying red cedars, another indication that this woodland was once a full-sunlight field. In a tiny field opening, poverty grass, or little bluestem, grows. Standing tall and blond throughout the winter, the new shoots shine blue, green, and even violet in early summer. On your left grows a clump of smooth sumac and bayberry bushes. Around 1980, the Nature Conservancy stopped mowing this field. Natural succession occurred, and it will not be much longer before the smooth sumac, bayberry, and poverty grass give way to shade-adapted woodland species.

At the T intersection, where bracken fern grows, turn right onto the Yellow Trail. Cross a stone wall. Note the cedar posts with the horseshoes. Cedar is resistant to decay, and, along with locust, was the popular post wood. Now backtrack 10 feet. Facing the cedar posts, on your right, grows a striped maple. Look in the woods and you'll see several more striped maples, whose seeds look like party decorations. Also known as moosewood, the green-striped trunk of this three-lobed, wide-leafed maple is more commonly seen to the north. Here it is near its southern range limit.

At the fork, bear left onto the Yellow Trail and keep left onto the White Trail; then turn left again onto the White Trail through a stone wall. Cross a brook, and emerge in open fields. This is what much of the property once looked like. Bear left for a walk to Weir Farm. The healthy, large, symmetrical red cedars have been trimmed around the bottoms of their trunks as high up as hungry deer can reach. Red cedar seedlings proliferate along the field edge. Cedar is one of the four sacred plants of Native America, used for ceremonial purification. European Americans of the old farming days gathered the blue cedar berries to ferment with sugar and grain into sockknocking gin. Also called juniper, the aromatic red heartwood of cedar is built into chests and closets to repel clothes moths. The volatile oil that repels the insects also inhibits the stomach bacteria in deer who crop the foliage. Red cedar can comprise up to 20 percent of a deer's total food intake with no ill effect. But when juniper reaches 30 percent of the deer's total food intake, proper digestion and nutrient absorption can no longer occur. A deer with a full stomach of juniper will starve to death.

Listen for the clown-like laugh of the pileated woodpecker. Large as a crow, these birds are flashy, with a red crest like Woody Woodpecker. They hammer old wood in dead trees as they forage for insects.

Walk down the dirt driveway to the red house. On your left is a planted row of northern white cedars. Unlike red cedar, the scales on these leaves are flattened. Once used for shipbuilding, these trees were commonly planted beside turn-of-the-century cemeteries.

Return to Weir Preserve the way you came, and continue left on the White Trail. Within the next two fields you can look for Virginia mountain mint to rub between two fingers for a refreshing smell. Slightly off center within the second field is a farmer's rock pile hidden beneath an island of shrubs. Shagbark hickory trees line the field's left edge. This White Trail leads you back to the map board. A left turn onto the Yellow Trail returns you to your car.

Devil's Den

Location: Weston, Connecticut
Distance: 2.8 miles
Owner: The Nature Conservancy

Devil's Den is so named because a hoofprint-shaped mark appears on a rock adjacent to one of its trails. Turn-of-the-century charcoal makers said the mark had been burned in by the Devil's hot feet. This large preserve has so many interesting trails you will want to return many times. The preserve is open 365 days a year, sunrise to sunset. There is no admission charge, but visitors are urged to make a contribution or to join the Nature Conservancy.

Access

From the Merritt Parkway, take Exit 42. Go north on CT 57 for 5 miles. Turn right onto Godfrey Road. Go 0.5 mile and turn left onto Pent Road, which dead-ends in the preserve's parking lot.

Trail

From the parking lot, walk around the road loop past the yellow-marked trail to the westernmost path, a wide road blocked by a wooden gate. This is the Pent Trail. Each trail intersection is marked by a large post with a number. At Post 3, bear left onto McDougal Trail; then bear left again at Post 17. This is the Saugatuck Trail.

One of the abundant plants along the way is hog peanut. This fragile trailing vine has small white or pale lavender flowers that form pods, each with several seeds. These seeds are not edible. However, the plant also has a single flower at the base of its stem. This flower develops a single, edible seed below the ground's surface, as do peanuts.

Two very successful practices at Devil's Den prevent you from slipping on log crossings over streams. Preserve workers top the logs with chicken wire or score them with a saw. You can still retain your footing even if the logs are wet.

Cross the west branch of the Saugatuck River on a wooden bridge. The water is very brown, probably from the high tannin content. It is also very clear and inviting. Saugatuck is an Indian word that means "outlet of the tidal river."

Keep straight, passing Post 14 on your right. On both sides of the trail grows the delicate, three-leafed dewberry, a blackberry that crawls along the ground. In June black-wing damselflies flutter weakly from perch to perch. When they are young, these beautiful insects live in the water of streams and rivers. The male has a bright turquoise body while the female has a black body and a white wing spot.

Cross the Saugatuck on a log bridge. Continue straight on the

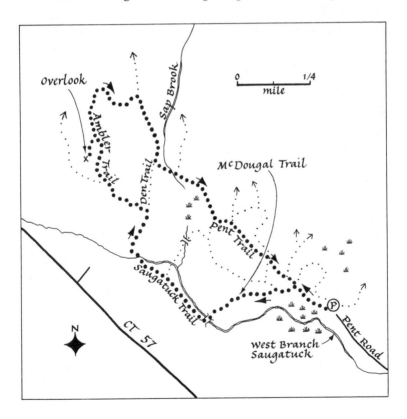

Only the passage of an occasional plane mars the feeling of remote wilderness at Devil's Den.

marked trail. Cross a stone wall and turn right. Turn left at Post 12. Search the logs along the trail for powderhorn lichen. There are three kinds of lichens: crustose, foliose, and fruticose. Crustose lichens hug the substrate closely. Foliose lichens, such as rock tripe (of which you will see a lot in this preserve), may be attached at only one point. Rock tripe looks like hideous scabs of toadskin. Fruticose lichens have upright, spore-bearing stalks, as in this powderhorn.

Bear right at Post 46, where the trail is bordered by mountain laurel and sweet pepperbush. Mountain laurel grows in well-drained soil, but pepperbush grows in wet soil. This seemingly unusual combination of bush species is actually quite common in this region where bedrock close to the soil surface traps water that saturates the soil in pockets amid the dry soil. Notice how the pepperbush disappears as soon as you climb the stairs to well-drained soil. At Post 45, turn left to walk out onto an overlook. Pitch pine grows here, with three needles in each cluster. Wintergreen and reindeer lichens grow along the side of the trail.

Go back to Post 45 and bear left. In July you can nibble your way along through lowbush blueberries. Huckleberry is here, too, but its fruits ripen a little later.

The pines on this exposed rocky ridge are pitch pines. A large patch of moss on the left of the trail has reindeer lichens mixed in and clumps of Indian pipe in summer.

Copperhead snakes inhabit this ridge, so beware. Copperheads are a beautiful coppery-brown in color, with darker brown milkbone shapes across their backs, solid-color heads, and bright pink tongues. They are venomous but not as dangerous or aggressive as rattlesnakes. One crawled past me, about three feet away, and slid into a crevice where I saw two more. Just watch where you put your hands and feet.

The trail descends into a beautiful gorge with a stream rushing along through rocks. Another uncommon plant that is found in several places along these lower trails is Indian cucumber root. Its flowering stalk stands above a whorl of leaves. Three blossoms are dependent below three more leaves. They hang down in order to be readily available to bumblebees, their pollinators, which cruise close to the ground looking for flowers. After the flowers are pollinated, the stalks straighten up above the top leaves, and dark blue berries form. The name indicates that the root of this plant is edible. Perhaps that is one reason it is not common.

Turn right at Post 44, then left at Post 10. This trail takes you back to Pent Trail and straight back to the parking lot.

Other Devil's Den trails have interesting things to see, such as an exhibit to show how charcoal was once made, a widespread and dangerous occupation in the 1800s. There is also an abandoned portable sawmill site; the mill was hauled through the woods on a large sled by a team of horses.

Seth Low Pierrepont State Park

Location: Ridgefield, Connecticut
Distance: 3 miles
Owner: State of Connecticut

Pleasant views across Lake Naraneka, specimen trees, and a steep trail to a high ridge with unusual vegetation are among the attractions of Pierrepont State Park. Walking a loop is possible, but only by spending some time tramping paved roads. Doing so will give you the opportunity to visit Kiah S. Brook Refuge, a nearby nature sanctuary.

To the left of the parking area is a large patch of mayapple. The one-inch white flowers, hidden between pairs of umbrella leaves, are followed in late spring by yellow egg-shaped fruits, reputedly edible but of questionable taste. Mandrake root is another name for this wildflower. Bordering the parking area are large honey locust trees. The clumps of thorns on the trunks look vicious. Many of the thornless, fruitless, domesticated forms of the locust have been developed from this tree.

Access

From Ridgefield, take CT 35 north to CT 116, turn left, and follow CT 116 for 2 miles. Turn right onto Barlow Mountain Road. At the first intersection, turn left, still on Barlow Mountain Road (straight ahead becomes North Street). The Pierrepont entrance is on the left between two white posts. Parking.

Trail

Follow the White Trail from the parking area. Huge sugar maples grow near the trail, their ancient trunks pocked with hollows where branches have fallen and decay has taken place. These hollows make ideal homes

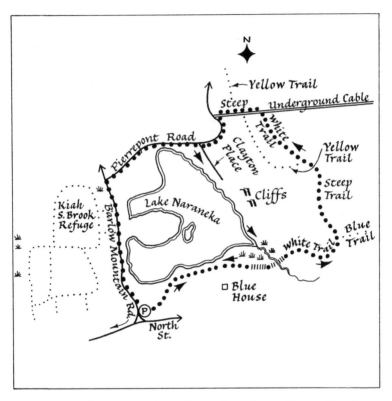

for raccoons, flying squirrels, and even honeybees. Ginger, bloodroot, and doll's eyes bloom here in spring. Later in the season blue lobelia enjoys the damp soil.

Where the trail curves left along the old stone wall and past a private blue house, there is a small forest of scouring rush. The trail, rather worn, has many exposed roots. In several places there are short spurs that lead to the edge of the lake. Mute swans, beautiful European additions to the area's bird population, nest on the lake in the spring. The adults can be seen with their gray cygnets from late spring until ice up.

Silt is filling in the lake where the stream enters. When Kaye Anderson first wrote this chapter in the mid-1980s, she described this as an area of open water blooming with arrowhead, wild mint, and mad-dog skullcap flowers. Within the decade, however, natural processes have taken over. The stream carried sediments, which were dumped at the lake mouth. Aquatic and shoreline plants died, decayed, and formed more silt. Natural succession occurred. You can clearly see this ongoing development of sunlight-to-shade and wet-to-dry soil species as you walk upstream: waterfront sedges come first, followed by cattails, then alders, until, finally, the area becomes a red maple swamp.

Logs have been placed in the wettest places to aid your passage. At the end of this corduroy bridge, the trail turns right. Most of the trees at this lower elevation are red and sugar maples, tulip trees, and dying ash. The great, tall, straight tulip trees had many historic uses. The fat ones could be burned into dugout canoes; the younger ones made superb ship masts.

The Blue Trail forks right, but continue walking on the White Trail as it turns left uphill. The swamp you have just passed on your right is grown with a shrub layer of spicebush. The trail begins to wind upward and at one point is very steep. A few laurel appear, with red and chestnut

Connecticut residents can get permits to launch boats for fishing on Lake Naraneka.

oaks, red maple, and black birch. There are a number of striped maples—the younger trees have green-striped bark and large leaves in the shape of a goose's foot. These striped maple, also called moosewood, are at the extreme southern limit of their range here at Seth Low Pierrepont State Park. Farther north they become quite common. They are found on the cooler, higher ridges of this park, where the climate most closely imitates their northern home.

The Yellow Trail forks left while you remain straight on the white. When this land was farmland there were probably views from this ridge over the lake. Now trees mask the lake in summer. The trail reaches an open area that has been cleared for an underground telephone cable. Here is a chance to see some of the flowers, such as goldenrod, that prefer meadow situations. Turn left and follow the clearing steeply downhill. Where the road turns right into the woods and onto private property, continue straight past boulders to Pierrepont Road. Turn left onto the paved road, then left again onto Clayton Place.

Along the left side of the road are tall plants of figwort, a member of the snapdragon family. The flowers are not spectacular, shiny green outside and brown inside, but they are best appreciated with a hand lens. The figwort blooms in late May and June. Soapwort, or bouncing bet, can also be found along this road in late summer. Soapwort was used in colonial times to make suds for washing clothes. It is still used to gently clean old fabrics and tapestries.

Return to Pierrepont Road and follow it to a left turn onto Barlow Mountain Road, circling Lake Naraneka. On your right is Kiah S. Brook Refuge. This is a good preserve for botanizing. The property is mostly wooded with red and sugar maple, red oak, and stands of red cedar, white pine, and spruce, interspersed with many field openings. This sort of mosaic of edges between fields and conifer and deciduous forests makes for good birding. There are several loops to enjoy. Wend your way back to Barlow Mountain Road, and your car, near the intersection with North Street.

Mayapple

Bear Mountain Reservation

Location: Danbury, Connecticut
Distance: 1.5 miles
Owner: City of Danbury

Nearly 100 acres of woodland and abandoned pasture have been preserved on this property that abuts Candlewood Lake but is composed mostly of slope and hilltop. This land has been made available for walkers to explore and enjoy by a joint project of the City of Danbury, the National Park Service, the Connecticut Department of Parks and Recreation, and a grassroots force of volunteers.

Access

If eastbound on I-84, take Exit 5 and follow signs for CT 37 north. If westbound on I-84, take Exit 6 and turn right onto CT 37 north. Follow CT 37 north 2 miles past the state prison and turn right onto Bear Mountain Road. The park entrance is 0.3 mile on the right. Parking.

Trail

Pick up a trail leaflet at the bulletin board. The John F. Kennedy Hiking Trail begins through a metal gate past the burned stone foundation of a barn. Follow the red blazes for the entire walk. Go down a short slope past multiflora rose bushes on your left and hairy vines of poison ivy climbing the trees on your right. Both of these plants grow berries. Multiflora rose, as its name implies, blooms multitudes of sweet-smelling pink and white flowers in early summer that ripen into multitudes of red rose hips. To try one of these vitamin C–laden fruits, remove the yellow seeds and eat the red skin only. They taste like fruit rollups—delicious. Rose hips are processed into commercial jams, teas, and vitamin C pills. Lovely though it may be, multiflora rose is an alien pest, brought to

America from Eurasia, that clogs farmers' fields and roadways. It creates excellent cover and food for birds and mammals, however.

Poison ivy blooms are nondescript white-green flowers that ripen into white berries. They are rarely seen because they are a major wildlife food eaten by nearly every bird and even some mammals, such as fox. They usually get snapped up in no time at all. They are inedible for humans.

Past the second small field the trail crosses a stream. Bear right at the fork. On your left is a tamarack plantation. Alien to this area, tamarack, or larch, is a deciduous conifer—normally a contradiction in terms—whose soft needles are arranged on the twig in whorls. Come fall the needles turn golden yellow and drop, to be replaced the following spring.

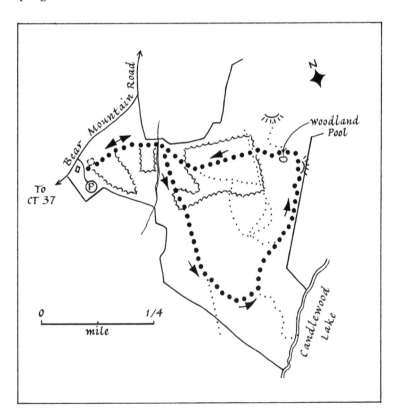

The trail soon emerges into a successional field of goldenrod. Sixty-nine species of goldenrod grow in the Northeast. Goldenrod pollen is so heavy it cannot be lifted by winds, so none of those 69 species causes hay fever unless, perhaps, you walk right through it. In August, how many different types of goldenrod can you find in this field? At first glance, the entire field is just yellow flowers. Look closer, however, and there is one with sprays arranged like a trumpet, there's another with stars of blossoms along one central stalk, and there's another flat as a tabletop. A careful eye will discover a plethora of yellow-bodied spiders and insects specially adapted to habitation in the goldenrod jungle.

You might find swollen globes within the forest of goldenrod stems. These are called insect galls. The female of a particular species of fly, midge, or tiny wasp alights on a particular part of a particular species of goldenrod in a process that is very species specific. She lays an egg and flies off. The egg causes a chemical reaction in the plant, and the goldenrod grows the gall around the egg. Some galls are spherical, others elliptical, but each species of insect creates a gall of a particular shape. Within the gall's central, hollow egg chamber, the insect matures, drills its way out, and flies off. Woodpeckers know what can be found in a gall and will peck it open to get at the grub. Old-time ice fishermen also knew about galls and could procure fresh "worms" in the middle of winter.

Within this successional field—by that I mean a field that is naturally succeeding to forest—grow two conifers: white pine and red cedar. White pine is the long-needled evergreen growing on the slope. The needles are actually held in bundles of five, one each for the five letters in "white" (one way to remember the name of the tree). White pine sap bleeds white. These white pine were probably planted and have spread through natural seeding. As one travels farther north, white pine occurs wild and becomes an important and dominant tree within the New England forest.

Red cedar or juniper's needles are actually scales. Red cedar is a field-colonizing species that grows swiftly in the open sunlight, a harsh, dry environment of wide temperature fluctuations that many other tree species cannot survive. Shade is cast beneath the junipers, and humidity is trapped. Their own young, who need full sunlight, cannot grow in that humid shade. Instead, shade-tolerant oak and sugar maple sprout and thrive. The oak and maple trees grow taller than the juniper, overtop them, shut out their full sunlight, and eventually kill them. This is no sad thing, however. It is the natural process called succession. A short moment in the sun is the red cedar's niche as a field pioneer species.

Continue straight on the red-marked trail through woods of ash and many oaks: red, black, white, and chestnut. Oak leaves with pointed lobes are red or black oaks; those with rounded but deep lobes are white oaks; those with only a wavy margin are chestnut oaks.

Watch for the fork where the red-marked trail turns left to meander through boulders and granitic bedrock outcrops. These rocks make for good climbing. The soil becomes drier, and, correspondingly, you will see fewer moist-slope red, black, and white oaks and more dry soil–adapted chestnut oaks. Other indicators of dry soils appear on one knoll: the presence of lowbush blueberry and huckleberry and the shorter oak trees. This dry upland soil condition is called xeric.

There is a distant view of Candlewood Lake through the trees in winter. The right turnoff onto the white-marked trail is a spur that leads downhill toward the lake. The red-marked trail continues along the ridge crest.

After passing through a small stand of mountain laurel, you will come to the overlook, where you can rest on the smooth bedrock to inspect the growth of lichens and mosses without the need to trample them. Lichens are actually two organisms from different kingdoms, a fungus and an alga, living together in harmonious symbiosis. (An alga and a fungus took a-lichen to each other, the saying goes.) The fungus strands provide the plant structure; the algae spots do the photosynthesizing. Lichens come in three different styles: crustose (crusty), foliose (leafy), and fruticose (having weird, bulbous, fairylike cups of fruiting bodies). Lichens usually begin the process of terrestrial succession. Exuding a weak acid against the rock and trapping dust beneath their lobes, these organisms build up the thinnest veneer of soil. Once there's enough soil, mosses take over, often growing right on top of the lichens (and killing them). Mosses trap even more dust, and decayed moss bodies hold even more water, making the soil layer thick enough for grasses to grow. Eventually, a field flourishes where once stretched only bedrock. The area's landscape is underlain by bedrock, all of which was soil-less and

*This woodland pool dries up at the end of the summer,
then refills with rainwater each spring.*

completely exposed bare rock 12,000 years ago when the Wisconsin Glacier receded. However, 12,000 years has not been time enough for soil to cover this slab of bedrock upon which you rest. Yet, succession is occurring. The layer of foliose lichen is thick, and mosses are growing. Within cracks where soil has accumulated more quickly, grasses and young trees are sprouting. How many more centuries will elapse before this boulder lies beneath woodland?

Resuming the walk, you will pass a vernal woodland pool. Some vernal pools fill with water only during times of heavy rain (usually in spring); others keep their water year-round. The trail leaflet supplied by the park calls this wetland a seasonal bog. Sometimes folks use the word bog to mean any wet place. However, a bog is something quite specific: It is a steep-sided, permanent pool with no inlet or outlet, usually formed when a chunk of glacial ice melted, that grows characteristic flora such as sedges, heaths, and sphagnum moss.

This seasonal woodland pool is the breeding center for wood frogs, toads, spring peepers, spotted and Jefferson salamanders, and fairy shrimp. Come June, the amphibian larvae have either matured and fled or died, and the fairy shrimp larvae have matured and burrowed for the remainder of the year into the pool mud. The pool slowly dries until all that is left is a black mat of dried dead leaves. Rains will refill the pool the following spring. The first steamy, warm, rainy night of spring brings about a mass movement of amphibians back to the pools of their birth, as did their parents, and their parents before them, and on down the ancestral line. They all return on one night, in the mist and the rain, to lie in writhing mats of mass mating orgies.

Just what is a wetland doing on top of a hill, though? Surrounded by xeric conditions, the vernal pool has red maple trees, highbush blueberry, and cinnamon ferns—all swamp species. The bedrock of the hilltop, however, forms a bowl that traps and holds rainwater. The diversity of a xeric and wetland habitat juxtaposed makes this a valuable area for use by wildlife, especially birds, who usually require more than one habitat to complete their life histories.

Sit on the rocks by the pool to gaze at tree reflections. Peer into the water for insect or jelly globes of frog eggs. Listen to the wind in the trees.

For a short side trip, take the white-marked trail on the right that leads uphill after a second right to a lichen-coated bedrock outcrop. When the leaves are down, you'll have a view of the surrounding countryside. Otherwise, stay on the red-marked trail, which circles the vernal pool and heads toward an open field. Before you reach the field, the trail is littered with tulip tree flowers in early summer (snipped by squirrels) and by tulip tree seeds blown down by the wind in autumn.

Emerge into the field. Notice the gray birches growing along the field's edge, leaning toward the sunlight. Gray birch, like red cedar, is a field pioneering species. The oldest trees grow at the wood's edge, the younger seedlings grow in the field. Over the years, then, the forest will appear to grow into the field, slowly shrinking it.

Go straight across this field, heading for the tamarack trees where you began your walk. Watch for deer beds in the grasses where deer have rested.

Pootatuck State Forest

Location: New Fairfield, Connecticut
Distance: 9.5 miles
Owner: State of Connecticut

Pootatuck, a word in a New England Algonquian language, translates into "country around the falls" or "country around the falls in the river" or "good fishing place," according to Trudy Lamb-Richmond of the Institute for American Indian Studies. When Europeans arrived, they named the Native People living at Pootatuck after the place. Now you hear of the tribal group of the Pootatuck people who lived in Woodbury, Southbury, New Milford, and on both banks (although especially the eastern bank) of the Housatonic River. The Pootatuck are closely related to the Paugussett. This state forest is part of their original homeland and its hills were used for hunting.

Swallow a last drink of water or fill your canteen at the spring across Short Woods Road. It is a good idea to carry a supply of water and food because this is a hike, not a stroll.

Access

Take Exit 6 off I-84 in Danbury. Take CT 37 north 3.5 miles. Turn right onto CT 39 east for 3 miles. Turn left at the sign for Squantz Pond State Park onto Short Woods Road. Continue 0.3 mile to a right turn into the main entrance of Squantz Pond State Park. There is a small parking lot at the trailhead beside the entrance booth. In winter, use the winter entrance for parking.

From the center of Sherman, drive south on CT 39 for 5 miles. Turn right at the sign for Squantz Pond State Park.

Trail

The trail begins by traversing old pastures that look like lawns in the fall. Climb the hill slope, paralleling Short Woods Road. The trail is not really a beaten path; you need to watch for the brown-and-white trail signs. As you climb you will have views of Squantz Pond, named for the Schaghticoke chief who lived nearby in the 1720s. The $5 million project that created Candlewood Lake for Connecticut Light and Power in the 1920s also increased the original size of half-mile-wide Squantz Pond four times. The steep-edged hills bordering the left bank of the pond are all Pootatuck State Forest hills.

The stratification of tree species is made apparent by leaf color in the fall. The red oaks turn bronze and golden on the crests and upper slopes, while the birches and tulip trees of the lower slopes flame yellow. The olive-green evergreens growing on the first and second hills are hemlocks. The third, lower hill is populated by bright green white pines. This is Pine Ledge, near the northern limit of the state forest.

At the last field, the trail enters woods and passes a small, wet meadow between the trees, home of very tall nettles and two of the area's common ferns. On your left grows sensitive fern, also called bead fern because its spores, borne on a central spike between the leaves, are clustered like a multitude of brown beads. Even after the first frost has withered the leaves, the upright, spore-bearing stalks remain all winter and into the next summer. On your right grows bracken fern, or brake, also known as eagle claw because, as it unfurls, the leaf looks like a large bird's claw. Bracken fern spores are held under the leaflets' rolled edges. A worldwide species, the withered leaves of bracken fern were used by Europeans of poor means to stuff their mattresses; the fern was mowed along with grasses to make cattle-bedding straw for use in barns and stables.

Continue through the woods to a right turn across a bridge, and enter the state forest. You will find yourself on a road built by the Civilian Conservation Corps (CCC), complete with stone culverts and retaining walls. The forest's 969 acres were acquired by the state between 1920 and 1931. A CCC tent camp, Camp Hook, was established in 1933 just south of Short Woods Road. The camp employed out-of-work masons and carpenters, who developed the road and trail system for the park. The woods road travels along the ridge slope under sugar maple, tulip tree, black birch, red oak, and hemlock. Boulders, which line the slope, are talus—debris that has fallen from the old cliffs above as the result of the heaving action of millennia of freezes followed by thaws. Look closely

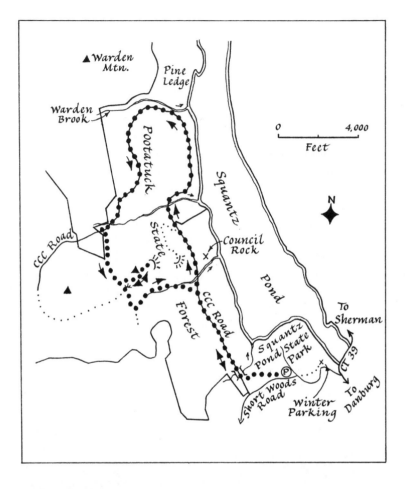

at the boulders you find beside the road. The outer surfaces of the rocks become weathered to a homogenous gray, but if you find a boulder with an underside protected from the weather, you will see the pink feldspar and white quartz crystals that identify it as granite. These rocks are part of the same Precambrian belt of ancient granitic-gneiss rocks that run west to the Hudson Highlands and then southwest into the Jersey Highlands.

The talus makes for fabulous exploration into nooks and crannies and cave overhangs. Ferns and woodland plants sprout on top of boulders and out of crevices. And, if you look closely at the rocks themselves, you will see the fairyland forms of multitudes of lichens and mosses. Some are wispy, some are crusty, some are like miniature ferns, and some are arranged in intricate rosettes. The more you look, the more you see. A plethora of different species, shapes, and colors lead to an incredible microexploration. The roadbed itself contains lichens and mosses colonizing the compacted dirt.

Rock tripe grows on some of the cliff bedrock faces and boulders. This lichen looks like toad skins or hung bats, but it's actually a family of foliose lichens that grow on acidic rocks. When wet, it resembles limp green-brown leather; when dry, it is brittle. Underneath it is black. Lichens are extremely sensitive to air pollution, especially sulphur dioxide. The last century has seen a severe decline in lichen distribution, incidence, and numbers. This decline is directly attributable to air pollution. Spectacular filamentous lichens draped like hairy beards on the trees can no longer be found; nor will you find rock tripe smothering cliffs.

Rock tripe is highly susceptible to vandalism. Idle walkers can't seem to resist pulling the "funny scabs" from the rocks, but rock tripe does not easily grow back. A rock tripe specimen begins as a pinhead. One that

This view of Candlewood Lake rewards the climb from meadows around Squantz Pond.

measures a foot across is centuries old. Enjoy the rock tripe, but never pick it. The profusion of rock tripe at Pootatuck State Forest means that the air is relatively pure and the area is free of vandalism.

Pass a trail on your left (your return loop), marked by wooden posts. Cross a sylvan stream under cool and moist hemlock woods. Down on the east slope lies the Council Rock of the Pootatuck. Although it is not visible from the trail, it is well worth mentioning. The Native groups of ancient Quinneticut had a traditional Council Rock, selected for the spiritual purity of the area, where political leaders or sachems met. Council Rocks were also used for religious and ceremonial purposes. This Council Rock is not one single rock but actually a series of cathedral-like caves.

A side trail on the right leads steeply uphill, through mountain laurel and hemlock to an overlook with views of Squantz Pond, Candlewood Lake, hills, and housing. If you've had enough walking, you may want to end your walk here and backtrack to the parking area.

If you're in for the entire hike, save your energy for the climb toward the end, when we'll get a similar overlook from higher up, though not quite so wide a view. Continue on the road as it wends its way through the woodland for 5 miles. The road crosses another gorgeous stream, then goes downhill and along the slope closer to the water. At a third stream crossing, the road climbs back uphill. It then curves away from Squantz Pond, parallels the waterfalls of talus-choked Warden Brook, and gradually climbs uphill. If you want to explore, you can cross the brook and bushwhack onto Pine Ledge. Otherwise, remain on the road as it bends southward. After about 1 mile you will come to a stream crossing. About 100 feet beyond this crossing is a left turn onto a narrow trail, marked by a silver-weathered post. If you miss the intersection, you will soon see a square stonework pool filled with water on your right. Turn around and go back to the turnoff.

The side trail leads through woodland. Turn left at the T intersection. On your left lies a small wetland within a hollow. Within about 100 feet, where the wetland ends, a narrow side trail leads into the sweet pepperbush on your left. Follow this path, climbing steeply uphill to the summit and a view through the trees. You will be within a crest woodland environment of white pine, chestnut and scrub oaks, lowbush blueberry, and huckleberry. This association of plants is adapted to the harsh, dry, xeric conditions of mountaintops where bedrock lies close to or at the thin, dry soil surface. Note how short and twisted the trees grow. The air smells of resin.

Continue over the hilltop and down the other side into a hollow. As soon as the trail dips into this area of deeper, more moist soil, the red oaks spring up tall and straight. The path climbs back up onto another small crest top into crest vegetation. It is here that you finally get your reward: a magnificent view of Squantz Pond, Candlewood Lake, and the hilly Connecticut countryside.

Return the way you came to a left turn onto the main trail and follow it downhill. The left side of the woods road is lined with blackberry. Watch on your left for a sign nailed to an oak tree that explains the timber-cutting technique of "Shelterwood Harvest." Turn left at the sign, and follow downhill through the thick growth of saplings that are reforesting the logged area. The road narrows to a path and leads steeply downhill. In spring this path practically becomes a streambed. Turn right at the T intersection. You will once again be on the CCC road and headed back to your car.

Putnam Memorial State Park

Location: Redding, Connecticut
Distance: 1 mile
Owner: State of Connecticut

One of the oldest state parks in Connecticut, Putnam is maintained as a memorial to an encampment of revolutionary war soldiers under the leadership of General Israel Putnam during the winter of 1778–1779. The statue of the general was made by Anna Hyatt Huntington when she was in her nineties. It shows the general, during one of his escapes from the British, riding his horse down steps cut into a cliff. (Other sculptures by this noted artist can be seen at the nearby Huntington State Park, Walk 35). While this park is not considered a "nature" park, there is much for a nature lover to see.

Access

From the Merritt Parkway, take Exit 45 for CT 58 (Blackrock Turnpike). Follow CT 58 for 13.8 miles to its intersection with CT 107. Bear left at the triangle, and enter the park at the statue of Israel Putnam. Park along the road inside the park.

Trail

Leave your car anywhere along the dirt road. Climb the hill to the fork and turn right. The first thing you will notice are piles of stones along the left of the road. These stones are the remnants of chimneys and fireplaces from wooden huts that sheltered the soldiers. Each 14-by-16-foot hut held from 8 to 12 soldiers. When they lived here, the entire area must have been barren of trees, for all wood was needed to keep warm and make cooking fires. Now the slopes are clothed with the typical oaks,

General Putnam's British opponent sent the general a new hat to replace the one with a bullet hole after this escapade.

hickories, and ashes of this climate. On the right you will see stairs to a museum. Check to see if this museum is open—it contains interesting exhibits, and a map that explains what each of 11 numbered posts commemorates may be available. Return down the stairs to the main path and continue.

Where a sign on your right directs you to a roadway entrance to the museum, turn left onto a narrow, slightly overgrown dirt path past a chimney. Pickerel frogs jump before you, disappearing in puffs of mud in the puddles along this path. The path climbs to a hillside of jumbled rocks where caves may have provided some additional shelter. These are not really caves but are more like shallow rock shelters. Certainly the hill itself would have helped keep the winter wind from the huts below. An old, decaying railing—be careful not to lean on it—helps you make your way along the front of this slope.

There is some jewelweed near the end of this path. While the rocky path provides a good place to watch migrating birds in spring, the jewelweed is where you should look for hummingbirds during fall migration. These tiny birds, weighing about two grams, must eat half their weight each day in order to fuel their active bodies. Most of this energy comes from nectar, but some comes from tiny insects and spiders.

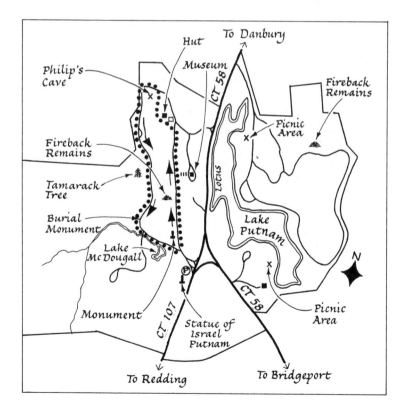

On chilly nights or rainy days, hummingbirds go into a state of torpor, during which their body temperatures and heartbeats slow down. Being in this inactive state is the only way they can survive to another day. Hummingbirds, indigenous to the New World, increase their weight by 50 percent before taking off for their long migration, which carries them to Mexico and Central America. The ruby-throated is the only hummingbird in the Northeast.

At the end of the cave path, turn left onto the dirt road once more. Occasional unmarked footpaths branch off. These footpaths seem to have been made by revelers and rock climbers and don't go very far. On the right side of the road, before a stone wall that lines the left side, are some young tamarack trees. The tamarack, or larch, is the area's only deciduous conifer. Its needles grow in tufts and are of the softest green, turning to gold in late fall before they drop to the ground.

The road continues, with a monument on the left marking the site where 15 soldiers who died during the encampment are buried. On the right is a small pond with dragonflies and whirligig beetles.

Return to your car, drive out of this section of the park, and go left onto CT 58. Turn right after about 0.5 mile to enter the other part of Putnam Memorial Park, which surrounds Lake Putnam. The road running through this section has many places to pull off, several with picnicking facilities. The lake itself is beautiful, and it has a surprise that I have found nowhere else in the area—American lotus. This handsome water plant has large pleated leaves, yellow flowers that look like silk, and big, round seedpods. Each seed is held in a hole in the seedpod's top. Such pods are often used for dried bouquets. Leaf, flower, and seedpod all stand a foot above the surface of the lake. Other plants in the water include white water lilies, blue pickerel weed, and arrow arum.

Collis P. Huntington State Park

Location: Redding, Connecticut
Distance: 4 miles
Owner: State of Connecticut

On a narrow country road, removed from major highways, Huntington State Park seems to be known mostly by people who live in its vicinity. Wide trails that are well maintained, beautiful woodlands, fields, and a large lake make it well worth a visit. The parking area entrance is graced by two statues sculpted by the noted wildlife artist Anna Hyatt Huntington, whose home this was. One statue depicts a mother bear with cubs; the other depicts a pair of howling wolves.

Access

From the Merritt Parkway, take Exit 45 to CT 58 (Blackrock Turnpike). Follow CT 58 for 10.9 miles. Turn right onto Sunset Hill Road. Continue 0.8 mile to the entrance on the right. Drive in and park on the grass.

Trail

On a clear day your first treat is a distant view of eastern Fairfield County's rolling hills. On the left of the parking area is a large field. Green in summer with waving grasses, in fall this field is a kaleidoscope of goldenrod and asters. Take the main path straight ahead, down the hill next to the field. At the fork, look to the right for a shrub with leaves that resemble black locust. This is not a sapling black locust but false indigo. In June it bears spikes of purple flowers with orange stamens, and in fall it has spires of short, brown seedpods. Though the identification books

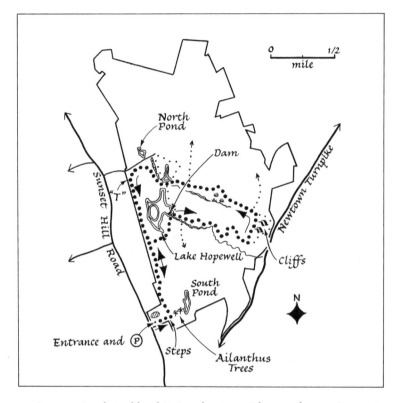

say it grows in places like this, in other areas I have only seen it next to rivers and salt marshes.

Turn left after descending some steps. Ailanthus trees rise across from the steps. Both sides of this trail are overgrown with wild grapes and are host to many alien species of plants. Bittersweet and multiflora roses make an impenetrable hedge on either side of the path. In fall privet's blue berries emerge here and there from this tangle. In spring old apple trees still bloom, their trunks pitted with holes of the yellow-bellied sapsucker.

Turn right at the first intersection. Suddenly the forest is made up of native trees and herbaceous plants. In spring these sugar maples are host to singing yellow-throated vireos. Look under laurel bushes along the left for patches of true wintergreen—the flavor of its leaves reminds me of teaberry gum. Its small, white flowers in late spring are followed by red berries in October. The path emerges onto Lake Hopewell's dam, with marsh St. Johnswort (the only pink member of its family) blooming among the rocks in September.

Turn right at the end of the dam, go downhill past white pine and mountain laurel, and take the left fork through deciduous woodland. A brook follows the trail on the right. Waves of ferns grow beneath the trees. There is much color variation between them, so these ferns can be identified with a bit of study. Most of the ferns here are hay-scented or New York. Both are a light yellow-green in color and both die down in the fall after turning rust and brown. Hay-scented fern is covered with a light silver fuzz and has a pleasant odor. New York fern has leaflets that taper at both ends of the frond. Occasional clumps of cinnamon and interrupted fern can also be found among these ferns. Cinnamon fern bears its spores on a separate stalk in early spring. There is always a tiny tuft of "cotton" at the base of each leaflet, if you look on the back, and the fern's stems are also very fuzzy. Interrupted fern, when it fruits, bears its spore capsules in the middle of the frond—thus "interrupted." It does not have the cotton tuft or so much fuzz on its stems.

Perhaps the easiest way to distinguish the ferns is to start with the evergreen ones. Some of these, such as Christmas and marginal shield fern, are very different in color from the herbaceous ferns. Christmas is dark green, and marginal shield is almost turquoise. Both have much thicker leaflets than do the hay-scented or New York ferns; thicker leaflets help them retain water during the hard days of winter.

Turn left, passing on your right a swamp with tupelo and sweet pepperbush—typical swampland plants—growing right beside mountain laurel, a plant of dry soils. You will see much of this sweet pepperbush, whose fragrant white flowers perfume the air in July and whose foliage graces the woodland with flaming reds and oranges come autumn. Listen for the crested flycatcher in the spring. Where the trail descends a short, steep slope into the fern hollow, the tall straight trees on your right are tulip trees.

Tall cliffs rise above the trail on the right. If you climb on top of these cliffs (go around to the back to find the side trail), you will find pitch pines growing out of the small amounts of soil trapped on the rock top. Pitch pine grows in the driest of habitats. Return to the main trail, where you will be bearing left at all forks all the way back to the lake. At the next left fork, start watching the swamp trees on the left. Wrist-thick, hairy poison ivy vines climb the trunks of many birches, ashes, and maples.

Poison ivy is one of the area's most common plants. It is also a versatile plant: As here, it can be a vine; in sandy soils it can be a shrub. Its leaves turn beautiful colors in the fall, and its small white berries are enjoyed by many birds, including flickers and yellow-rumped warblers, who distribute the seeds from its berries to new areas.

A stream flows downhill on your left as you follow the path through deciduous woodland, remembering always to bear left at forks. When you first see the lake, stay straight to the causeway between the two lakes. Standing at the larger lake's beach, you can see underwater the remains of a boathouse or dock. These remains date back to the late 1800s, when the land's owners kept a steam paddlewheeler on this lake. The boat is said to be lying under the water. If you are visiting in winter, look across the lake and you might see a small stone structure that looks like a lighthouse on an island.

As you cross a bridge between the main Lake Hopewell and its East Lagoon, look to your right for a second bridge. It is a nice place to sit and watch natural events. A friend and I sat here one day, eating lunch and throwing crumbs to the fish below. We heard splashing around a bend in the cove, and suddenly an osprey flew into view, bearing a large fish in its talons. Since it was late June, this brought us hope that the once-endangered bird might be breeding nearby.

Do not cross this second bridge, but go back and continue on the main trail. In August look across the East Lagoon to see swamp mallow blooming.

When the trail reaches a T intersection, turn left. Dame's rocket, a member of the mustard family with one-inch, fragrant, white-to-lavender flowers, blooms here from May into the summer. It makes a pleasant garden flower, and I have found that if I cut some at home for a bouquet, side shoots develop and extend the plant's blooming season. Please do not take any plants from the park; you can find Dame's rocket along many roadsides.

This wide path traverses the area that must have been used for farm animals when the Huntingtons lived here. Apparently, Anna Hyatt Huntington kept horses, cows, and other animals so that she could study them

It is doubtful that there is enough wilderness left east of the Hudson River to support black bears in the lower states.

for her statues. On the left, one stone building houses a huge boiler; another seems to have been a stable, perhaps for cows or pigs. Large sugar maples shade the dirt road. You almost expect to see a horse and carriage come along.

This road will take you back to the steps, where you will turn right, ascend the slope by the meadow, and return to your car. Or, while along the carriage road, you may take the second right turn up through the successional goldenrod field, climb the slope, and turn left at the top to return to your car.

Paugussett
State Forest

Location: Newtown, Connecticut
Distance: 4.5 miles
Owner: State of Connecticut

Paugussett State Forest is split into two properties. This walk covers the south parcel only. The north parcel is located off Hanover Road in the northern part of Newtown. Hunting is allowed, so be careful in the fall. It's a long walk, but the hemlock woods are enchanting and the place is big enough to give you the feeling that you're in the middle of wilderness.

The Paugussett, who once controlled Fairfield County and beyond, lived on both banks of the Housatonic River and are one of the four original Native Peoples of old Quinneticut. The others are the Mohegan, the Narragansett, and the Pequot. Paugussett might mean either "pond-small-at" or "swift current in the divided river" or "the river widens out where the fork joins," according to recent linguistic work. However, Chief Big Eagle of the Golden Hill Paugussett, who lives on America's smallest Indian reservation—¼ acre in Trumbull (and they've had to fight in recent years to keep it)—says the name means "narrows" or "crossing place." The people, therefore, named themselves after the place where they lived.

Access
Take Exit 11 off I-84. Turn right onto Mile Hill Road for 0.1 mile. Turn right onto CT 34 east 4.9 miles to a left turn onto Great Quarter Road. Drive 1.3 miles to the end. Parking.

Trail
The blue-marked Zoar Trail begins at the end of the parking circle. The Stevenson Dam flooded the Housatonic River downstream in 1919 to

form Lake Zoar. Before the dam was built, the river had eroded a steep-sided gorge. Now the valley floor is drowned, and the hills don't seem as high. The trail leads along the lake and riverbanks under mixed deciduous and hemlock woods. The soil of the trail is sandy; it was

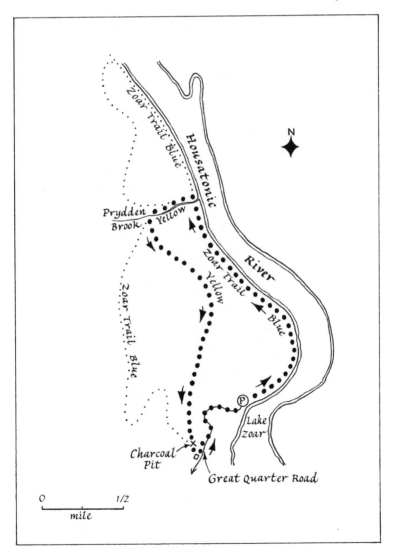

deposited there by the river. Take a quick jaunt over to the Housatonic itself to see the steep, sandy bank. Housatonic is a Mahican Indian word derived from *wassi* (which means beyond), *aton* (which means mountain), and *ic* (a locative place-name ending, although some say *ic* is a river ending for a word). Therefore, Housatonic means "area beyond the mountain" or "river beyond the mountain." This sounds like a Mahican way of describing a place beyond their homeland, and, indeed, the Mahican originally lived over the ridges in the Hudson Valley. Over time, they moved into the northern part of the Housatonic Valley.

As you walk these cool, moist woods, you will see two recurring ground plants: spotted wintergreen and princess pine. Spotted wintergreen (*Chimaphila maculata*), sometimes called spotted pipsissewa, stands no higher than a human hand. Its thick, deep green leaves are striped down the midrib by a white pattern. The serrated leaves are arranged in whorls around the single stem. Pipsissewa flowers, which bloom in August, are lovely: Small, waxy, white blooms nod from the tip of the stalk, with orange and green stamens and pistils in the center. It's well worth getting down on your hands and knees to smell them. These flowers mature into brown buttons by fall. You can find this plant at any time of year, even under snow. In fact, its genus name *Chimaphila* means winter-loving. You will not see it in profusion; it occurs here and there in small colonies of a few handsome, individual plants. As far apart sometimes as 10 feet, the individuals are actually part of the same plant connected to one another by extensive root systems.

Princess pine (*Lycopodium obscurum*) is a club moss that looks like a miniature pine tree. As with spotted wintergreen, groups of princess pine plants are actually all one plant attached by an underground runner. In early summer, the "pines" grow green candelabra, inside of which the spores ripen. By late summer the candelabra turn brown. The slightest waft of air stirs the tiny, dustlike reproductive spores loose on the wind. If they land in suitable habitat, these spores will grow into a different style of plant that looks like one tiny leaf. Folks rarely see these plants because they lack chlorophyll and are not green. They live in association with the soil fungi. Male and female cells within the leaf unite, and from them grows the club moss "pine," which begins a new colony. Ropes of club mosses were commonly gathered in wintertime for holiday decorations.

The flammable spores were also gathered for gunpowder, flash powder on cameras, and foot powder. Such collecting has contributed to the decline of this fascinating plant. Now and then throughout the state forest you might see two relatives of princess pine, the *Lycopodium* ground cedar and shining club moss.

The blue-marked trail parallels the river. Twice the blue marks jog off the main road to avoid mud, only to return after a short distance. The road ends at the charred remains of Mahar Cottage and a campsite. The narrow path then follows the steep Housatonic bank beneath hemlocks that, in late fall and winter, are populated by kinglets and slate-colored juncos.

Hemlocks grow and tend to persist on slopes in southern New England, where it is cool and moist year-round. In traditional ecological terms, such a growth is called a climax forest: self-perpetuating and stable, barring catastrophe (such as a blowdown or a bulldozer). It is so dark beneath their needles that few, if any, shrubs or herbaceous plants can grow. A dense hemlock canopy allows less than 20 percent of a day's full sunlight to penetrate to the forest floor. This lack of sunlight enhances humidity and coolness. In such shade only sapling and seedling hemlocks are found, but even they cannot flourish without sunlight. Although extremely shade-tolerant, a shaded hemlock grows slowly. Trees no thicker than a broom handle may be 50 years old. If a blowdown opens the overhead canopy to let in the full sunlight, that 50-year-old hemlock will shoot up, growing faster in a few summers than in all its 50 years. This is one of the adaptations that make hemlock a dominant species.

Hemlocks were heavily harvested in colonial times. Their bark, which is high in tannin, was stripped from the trees for use in the skin-tanning industry. Native peoples used hemlock for its astringent properties. Hemlock used as an astringent is stronger than a lemon. Hemlock tea bathed on a wound closes it and stops the bleeding. Hemlock needle tea puckers the mouth, the esophagus, the stomach lining, the intestinal lining, and is still strong enough to tighten the large intestine and stop severe diarrhea. Taken as a weak tea or munched raw, hemlock needles supply vitamin C.

The path leads downhill, across a brook, and back uphill. At the top where the path levels off, the creeping ground plant called partridgeberry grows on both sides of the trail. Tubular flowers ripen into red berries that are poisonous to partridges. As it heads downhill again, the trail joins a gully, which is actually an old road gullied by erosion. You will pass many of these old roads on this walk. All of them end at the river as if they keep going underwater. Indeed, before the valley was flooded, these roads went to the original banks of the Housatonic River.

Cross the second brook and enjoy views through the trees of the Housatonic. Twenty-five feet before you cross the third mountain brook grows a patch of rattlesnake plantain on your left. This wild orchid's ground rosette of leaves are dark green, checkered in yellow-white, and feel slightly rubbery. As with all orchids, the rattlesnake plantain survives through a mutualistic mycorrhizal association between its roots and the soil fungi. If the orchid is transplanted, the fungi will die and so will the rattlesnake plantain. Once the plant is sufficiently mature, it will send up a central spike adorned with tiny, exotic white orchids.

At the fourth brook, the little valley slopes are covered with Christmas ferns. Each leaflet looks like a Christmas stocking. As with princess pine, this evergreen fern was once extensively gathered during the winter holidays as a part of "bringing in the greens." Spores are borne at the ends of fertile fronds beneath miniature leaflets.

Now and then along the shore you might notice, in autumn, a shrub hung with papery bladders. This is bladder nut. Its leaves grow in groups of three, and the balloons hold the seeds that, when dried, rattle around inside the bladder when shaken. The trail leads to a small sandy beach with an open view of the opposite hills and rocks. This is a good place to sit for a rest and maybe sight a beaver. Unfortunately, the shores are strewn with water-borne garbage.

The trail crosses a brook and leaves the rivershore to head into a deep and dark hemlock forest crossed by clear brooks. At the old road fork, keep left on the blue-marked Zoar Trail. Downhill you will hear the splashing of the waterfall. Use the side trails or bushwhack through the open woods to the falls. The blue-marked trail crosses Prydden Brook above the falls, yet there is no bridge; you must pick your way across on stones. At the next fork, the blue-marked Zoar Trail continues right for a 2-mile loop. You may go that way or turn left onto the yellow-marked Prydden Brook Trail to cut off that loop. The yellow-marked trail climbs up the valley past waterfalls and cascades. Halfway up the valley, the blue-marked Zoar Trail rejoins the yellow-marked trail. As you continue uphill, soil moisture lowers and the hemlocks thin as the forest becomes a mixed deciduous species association. The blue-marked trail leaves the old road to run left across Prydden Brook.

Zoar Trail climbs a hill through a typical southwestern Connecticut oak crest woods mixed with black birch and beech and overrun with mountain laurel. At the top is a wintertime view through the trees of the surrounding ridges. You may bushwhack to rocks on your left for a view of the river below. At the next intersection, you may continue straight on the blue-marked trail for a longer way home up and over ridges; otherwise turn left onto the yellow-marked trail, which follows along the crest through hemlock stands, mixed oaks, and mountain laurel, past a red maple area where the bedrock traps rainwater and the soil is wet.

Mountain laurel is evergreen; the thick stands that occur in these woodlands provide good winter cover for birds and deer. Trying to walk through a stand of twisty-trunked laurel has given rise to its title of laurel hell.

Keep straight at the T intersection. You will be on the red-marked trail within a laurel hell. Slowly descend the escarpment within 0.75 mile to an intersection with the blue-marked Zoar Trail. Turn left onto an old road. On the left is a deep, round pit. This is a charcoal pit, dug perhaps during the early 1800s. Into this pit were stacked many cords of wood cut on the site by colliers, or charcoal-makers. Covered with soil and leaves, the stack was set on fire and allowed to smolder for weeks until the wood carbonized into charcoal. The colliers then sold their charcoal to the iron-smelting industry, steamship companies, and households.

Turn left at the paved road for a 0.5-mile tramp back to your car.

Let Backcountry Guides Take You There

Our experienced backcountry authors will lead you to the finest trails, parks, and back roads in the following areas:

50 Hikes Series

50 Hikes in the Adirondacks
50 Hikes in Connecticut
50 Hikes in the Maine Mountains
50 Hikes in Coastal and Southern Maine
50 Hikes in Maryland
50 Hikes in Massachusetts
50 Hikes in Michigan
50 Hikes in the White Mountains
50 More Hikes in New Hampshire
50 Hikes in New Jersey
50 Hikes in the Hudson Valley
50 Hikes in Central New York
50 Hikes in Western New York
50 Hikes in the Mountains of North Carolina
50 Hikes in Ohio
50 Hikes in Eastern Pennsylvania
50 Hikes in Central Pennsylvania
50 Hikes in Western Pennsylvania
50 Hikes in the Tennessee Mountains
50 Hikes in Vermont
50 Hikes in Northern Virginia

Walks and Rambles Series

Walks and Rambles on Cape Cod and the Islands
Walks and Rambles on the Delmarva Peninsula
Walks and Rambles in the Western Hudson
    Valley
Walks and Rambles on Long Island
Walks and Rambles in Ohio's Western Reserve
Walks and Rambles in Rhode Island
Walks and Rambles in and around St. Louis

25 Bicycle Tours Series

25 Bicycle Tours in the Adirondacks
25 Bicycle Tours on Delmarva
25 Bicycle Tours in Coastal Georgia and the
    Carolina Low Country
25 Bicycle Tours in Maine
25 Bicycle Tours in Maryland
25 Bicycle Tours in the Twin Cities and Southeast-
    ern Minnesota
30 Bicycle Tours in New Jersey
30 Bicycle Tours in the Finger Lakes Region
25 Bicycle Tours in the Hudson Valley
25 Bicycle Tours in Ohio's Western Reserve
25 Bicycle Tours in the Texas Hill Country and
    West Texas
25 Bicycle Tours in Vermont
25 Bicycle Tours in and around Washington, D.C.
30 Bicycle Tours in Wisconsin
25 Mountain Bike Tours in the Adirondacks
25 Mountain Bike Tours in the Hudson Valley
25 Mountain Bike Tours in Massachusetts
25 Mountain Bike Tours in New Jersey
Backroad Bicycling on Cape Cod, Martha's
    Vineyard, and Nantucket
Backroad Bicycling in Eastern Pennsylvania
Backroad Bicycling in Connecticut

Bicycling America's National Parks Series

Bicycling America's National Parks: Arizona &
    New Mexico
Bicycling America's National Parks: California
Bicycling America's National Parks: Oregon &
    Washington
Bicycling America's National Parks: Utah &
    Colorado

We offer many more books on hiking, fly-fishing, travel, nature, and other subjects. Our books are available at bookstores and outdoor stores everywhere. For more information or a free catalog, please call 1-800-245-4151 or write to us at The Countryman Press, P.O. Box 748, Woodstock, Vermont 05091. You can find us on the Internet at www.countrymanpress.com.